ƒ

M000082950

New Worshiping Communities

New Worshiping Communities

A Theological Exploration

Vera White and Charles Wiley

WESTMINSTER
JOHN KNOX PRESS
LOUISVILLE · KENTUCKY

© 2018 Vera White and Charles Wiley

First edition
Published by Westminster John Knox Press
Louisville, Kentucky

18 19 20 21 22 23 24 25 26 27—10 9 8 7 6 5 4 3 2 1

All rights reserved. No part of this book may be reproduced or transmitted in any form or by any means, electronic or mechanical, including photocopying, recording, or by any information storage or retrieval system, without permission in writing from the publisher. For information, address Westminster John Knox Press, 100 Witherspoon Street, Louisville, Kentucky 40202-1396. Or contact us online at www.wjkbooks.com.

Unless otherwise indicated, Scripture quotations, are from the New Revised Standard Version of the Bible, copyright © 1989 by the Division of Christian Education of the National Council of the Churches of Christ in the U.S.A., and used by permission. Scripture quotations marked CEB are from the Common English Bible, © 2011 Common English Bible, and are used by permission. Scripture quotations marked NLT are taken from the Holy Bible, New Living Translation, copyright 1996, 2004. Used by permission of Tyndale House Publishers, Inc., Wheaton, Illinois 60189. All rights reserved.

Book design by Drew Stevens
Cover design by Mary Ann Smith

Library of Congress Cataloging-in-Publication Data

Names: White, Vera K., author.
Title: New worshiping communities : a theological exploration / Vera White
    and Charles Wiley.
Description: Louisville, KY : Westminster John Knox Press, 2017. | Includes
    bibliographical references.
Identifiers: LCCN 2017047278 (print) | LCCN 2017048185 (ebook) | ISBN
    9781611648461 (ebk.) | ISBN 9780664263096 (pbk. : alk. paper)
Subjects: LCSH: Church development, New. | Church development,
    New—Presbyterian Church (U.S.A.) | Church. | Public worship.
Classification: LCC BV652.24 (ebook) | LCC BV652.24 .W45 2017 (print) | DDC
    285/.137—dc23
LC record available at https://lccn.loc.gov/2017047278

Most Westminster John Knox Press books are available at special quantity discounts when purchased in bulk by corporations, organizations, and special-interest groups. For more information, please e-mail SpecialSales@wjkbooks.com.

Contents

Acknowledgments

Collaboration is a word more familiar in concept than in practice. This volume is a product of genuine collaboration. The most important collaborators are the group of practitioners and scholars who we identify in chapter 1.

This was also a genuine collaboration for the two of us, representing two parts of the church's structure that have not always been at ease with one another: (1) evangelism and (2) theology and worship. While one of us is oriented more toward tangible results and the other toward abstract ideas, we both care deeply about the church and the world to which that church is called. Working together brought forth the best form of collaboration, where the final product was much better than what either of us could have produced on our own.

We want to thank David Maxwell for his patient and gentle leadership through nine (!) book proposals before we hit the mark.

We hope that this collaboration serves the Spirit's work to send us forth in mission as all things are reconciled in God.

Grace and peace,
Vera and Charles

Introduction

In the 1990s, something cracked in denominational new church development offices and programs. Leaders noticed conversations happening across the church, from some very unexpected places, about the nature of the church.

Something essential was changing about the church, and leaders struggled to understand or define it. Traditional church vocabulary gave no words for the phenomenon they were seeing: people of faith meeting under a bridge, a for-profit coffee shop that transformed into a church on Sunday evening, a busload of traveling artists and musicians pulling into a truck stop for a Communion service. Was this church? Who was in charge? Why was it happening? Conversations were buzzing, but mostly they seemed to be outside of the church building and church hours.

One professor at Pittsburgh Theological Seminary opened his home to a small group of seminary students, pastors, and ordinary people exploring a call to start what are now called new worshiping communities. They read and prayed together—and they talked.

A conversation by its very definition means that no one is the expert or the leader, that many voices need to be heard, that there is not a formula for shared work, that each person spends more time listening than talking, that there are more questions than answers. A conversation creates space to argue about things, even things we don't believe in, to try to get to the truth. We find that the truth is among us, but sometimes we can get at it only by argument, dissection, and passionate debate. A conversation is dynamic.

So when a group of theologians and practitioners came together at Pittsburgh Theological Seminary in November 2015 to talk about new worshiping communities, they engaged in conversation. This time the conversation centered on biblical and theological reflections on the new reality of church they were observing in their midst. This book reflects the results of that conversation. Conversation is where new worshiping communities incubate, and when it includes both theologians (those who think about church) and practitioners (those who engage in the work of the church), the conversation becomes rich and layered. A new level of accountability also develops. Experimentation and exploration become deeply grounded in theology; theology puts on its work clothes and takes to the streets.

WHAT IS IN THIS BOOK

What you will find in the pages ahead are the results of conversations among theologians and practitioners who have reflected deeply on the occurrence of new worshiping communities. Some of the participants have come to the table with skepticism about the very idea that church might need to take on new forms in this new century. The very idea of contextualizing the gospel is disconcerting. Others jumped in enthusiastically, even blindly, and began reflecting later.

These conversations are, of course, not limited to one denomination, one gathering, one language, or one nation. They are part of a much larger conversation in the church of Jesus Christ. The contributors to the conversations in this book all have deep connections to the Presbyterian Church (U.S.A.), not because we claim any predestined right to ownership of the movement but because we believe this denomination has something to say—that it represents one important strand of the conversation.

A NEW MOVEMENT

The PC(USA) jumped into the movement of missional church planting without a lot of reflection. Buoyed by our Protestant work ethic, our historical passion for engaging unchurched people, and a deep gratitude for the fresh expressions of God's presence in a complex and changing world, the PC(USA) launched the 1001 New Worshiping Communities initiative by action of its General Assembly in the summer of 2012—without a theological apologetic or a written manual but with loads of enthusiasm and energy.

Part of the genius of the 1001 New Worshiping Communities initiative is that we didn't try to figure everything out before we started. New church development in past decades had become so organizationally heavy and capital dependent that midcouncils and congregations were reluctant to start anything new. Most regional councils claimed at least one story of an expensive and embarrassing failure that led to many declarations of "We already tried that and it doesn't work."

This new movement started with a vision and encouragement to act. Now that several hundred new worshiping communities have been established, the need for a more robust theological framework is evident. We look back over the past few years and reflect on what God's Holy Spirit has been up to among us. This book is the result of some of our reflections. We believe that the PC(USA) has a word to say within the broader conversation. Because of its rich history of church planting around the world, the breadth of its Reformed theology, its tradition of inclusion, and its flexibility in worship expression, the PC(USA) is well-suited to play a role in contemporary church-planting experiments. Although we suspect that the primary audience for this book will be found among those who serve within the Reformed branches of the church, we hope that the story of what God is doing in our little corner of the church may be of interest to all those who are seeking to be faithful in a time of constant change.

A DEFINITION

Our starting point for the conversation is the definition that was developed at the beginning of the initiative in 2012. It's kind of odd to start out with a definition, but that's what we called it. The definition is an elaboration on three terms: *new, worshiping, communities.*

New

—Seeking to make and form new disciples of Jesus Christ
—Taking on varied forms of church for our changing culture

Worshiping

—Gathered by the Spirit to meet Jesus Christ in Word and sacrament
—Sent by the Spirit to join God's mission for the transformation of the world

Communities

—Practicing mutual care and accountability
—Developing sustainability in leadership and finances

The definition is short and simple and is not meant to be prescriptive. Taken as a whole, it assumes a core ecclesiology. New worshiping communities *are* church, not a shortcut or a substitute for the real thing. For those who participate in them, new worshiping communities contain all the elements of church. In the pages ahead, each of the bullet points in the definition will be fleshed out, dissected, and affirmed. The structure of the book loosely follows the order of the definition.

CONVERSATION PARTNERS

Conversation partners in this project include

—Christopher Brown, then serving as organizing copastor of the Upper Room and coordinator of the Church Planting Initiative, Pittsburgh Theological Seminary
—Darrell Guder, professor of missional and ecumenical theology emeritus, Princeton Theological Seminary
—Scott Hagley, assistant professor of missiology, Pittsburgh Theological Seminary
—Sara Hayden, associate for 1001 New Worshiping Communities, PC(USA)
—Libby Tedder Hugus, pastor of the Table in Casper, Wyoming
—Christopher James, assistant professor of evangelism and missional theology, University of Dubuque Theological Seminary
—Jin Kim, pastor of Church of All Nations, Columbia Heights, Minnesota

—Cynthia L. Rigby, W. C. Brown Professor of Theology, Austin Presbyterian Theological Seminary

—Edwin van Driel, Directors' Bicentennial Associate Professor of Theology, Pittsburgh Theological Seminary

—Vera White, coordinator, 1001 New Worshiping Communities, PC(USA)

—Charles Wiley, coordinator, Office of Theology and Worship, Presbyterian Mission Agency

—Steve Yamaguchi, dean of students and assistant professor of pastoral theology, Fuller Theological Seminary

Each chapter draws on the insights of one or two of these respected theologians and practitioners. Charles Wiley and Vera White have drawn upon the articles written by the other participants to shape this book, which provides an overview of the conversations. A collection of all the original articles in their entirety is forthcoming. When an extensive quotation is used, the presenter's name is in parentheses after the quotation.

Our hope is that you will use this book as a discussion starter for your own group to have a conversation about the current challenges and opportunities of the church of the twenty-first century.

1

Communities of Grace and Gratitude

What's the point?

That's what a lot of folks inside the church and outside the church are asking about Christianity, about church, about faith in Jesus Christ. And here we are talking about the importance of forming new worshiping communities, communities formed around Jesus Christ. What's the point?

New worshiping communities are not a technical fix to what is ailing the church. They are not a technique that any community can apply in order to flourish. New worshiping communities are a contextually appropriate way to embody the gospel of Jesus Christ in a world that needs this good news. Thus it is important that we spend some time reflecting on the nature of this gospel and how we communicate it and live it.

THE GOSPEL SUMMARIZED: GRACE AND GRATITUDE

So much of the way we talk about the church is small—not in terms of size but of vision. We end up talking about the nature of the church in ways that are not compelling, not life-changing. Our message is not big enough for our vision. How might we conceive of and practice church in a way that is compelling and life-changing? What emerges from the core of our identity that compels us to practice Christian community, proclaim the gospel, and work for justice?

We believe that the theme of *grace and gratitude* provides this compelling message. Grace and gratitude succinctly and winsomely describe the charism, the gift of the Reformed tradition. Within the church ecumenical, different traditions have gifts that they offer to the wider church. We in the Reformed movement learn the discipline of not conforming to the surrounding culture from the Mennonites, an appreciation for God's presence in the sacraments from Roman Catholics, a commitment to engage the structures of society from the National Baptists, and the exuberance of the Spirit from Pentecostals. Grace and gratitude are our gifts to the wider church.

This description comes alive in Brian A. Gerrish's book *Grace and Gratitude*, in which Gerrish explores John Calvin's theology of the Lord's Supper. At the table, the relation of God and humanity is exhibited. God calls us to the table and feeds us with Christ himself, and we are sent forth in gratitude for God's gracious movement toward us. The relationship broken by sin is restored at God's initiative—we offer our thanks with our whole lives. More than a characterization of Calvin's theology of the Lord's Supper, grace and gratitude are a simple yet deep description of Calvin's entire theological vision.

Grace and gratitude are our theological and spiritual vision. They give us an expansive vision of God. What is our picture of God? The gracious one who comes to us in creation, in the law, in the prophets, and ultimately in the person of Jesus Christ. The God who sustains us with the ongoing grace of the Holy Spirit. The God who calls us through the church. The God who is for us.

Grace

The grace of our Lord Jesus Christ be with you.

The apostle Paul greets worshiping communities with these words throughout his epistles. In a very real sense, this is a summary of the good news, the gospel, of Jesus Christ. God's grace has come to us in the person of Jesus Christ, a grace that is with us, is near to us, surrounds us.

We live in a time when grace is needed but isn't necessarily part of the everyday language of most people. Grace is important enough that we must try to recover its meaning. Grace expresses the character of God in a way that is especially important in our context where the church often functions as a symbol of guilt and obligation.

Why grace?

A profound articulation of grace comes from the French baptismal liturgy developed by the Huguenot church in the Reformation:

> Little one, for you Jesus Christ came into the world:
> for you he lived and showed God's love;
> for you he suffered the darkness of Calvary
> and cried at the last, "It is accomplished";
> for you he triumphed over death and rose in newness of life;
> for you he ascended to reign at God's right hand.
> All this he did for you, little one,
> though you do not know it yet.
> And so the word of Scripture is fulfilled:
> "We love because God loved us first."[1]

That is grace.

Be with You

What makes this such good news is that grace is directional rather than static. Paul's statement is also a blessing: "The grace of our Lord Jesus Christ be with you." It is the direction of God toward human beings before we ever thought to turn toward God. It is the movement of God toward us when we are moving away from God. It is the movement of God toward us when we are oblivious. It is the movement of God toward us when we don't care.

Grace comes to us in the person of Jesus Christ, the one who ate with sinners, welcomed children, and identified with the dispossessed. Grace comes to us, lives among us, envelopes us.

Transforming Grace

This grace that comes to us as we are does not leave us as we were. Our encounter with Jesus Christ transforms us. Reflecting on this mystery, the sixteenth-century church leader John Calvin spoke of grace as having a double effect.

The first effect is to take away our guilt from sin. For centuries, Christians have proclaimed the good news of the forgiveness of sins as unabashed good news. Everyone knew they were sinners. The question was whether they were saved from that sin. However, not everyone shares that common conviction now. In a real sense, we must begin with the profound gift of grace grounded in God's overflowing love for us. Over time, through the proclamation of the gospel, the Holy Spirit will work in the hearts of people so that they will begin to see the depth of their sin and become even more grateful for the grace shown to them in Jesus Christ.

The second effect is transformation. Grace takes away our guilt, but it also transforms us. In 2 Corinthians, Paul writes that those who are in Christ are new creations. This transformation isn't fast, unfortunately. While we may want everything now, it doesn't work that way. John Calvin used the image of crawling on our hands and knees. We get somewhere, but it isn't fast or without effort.

Gratitude

What is the appropriate response to grace? Gratitude. Gratitude for our lives, for our treasure, for our community. Gratitude that compels us to share the love of Christ in the community and to do justice and love mercy for all God's children. Karl Barth wrote, "[Grace and gratitude] belong together like heaven and earth. Grace evokes gratitude like the voice an echo. Gratitude follows grace like thunder [follows] lightning."[2] If God is, in essence, grace, then we are, in essence, gratitude.

We hear grace and gratitude in the last clause in Question 86 of the Heidelberg Catechism:

**Q. Since we have been delivered
from our misery
by grace through Christ
without any merit of our own,
why then should we do good works?**
A. Because Christ, having redeemed us by his blood,
is also restoring us by his Spirit into his image,
so that with our whole lives
we may show that we are thankful to God
for his benefits.[3]

The answer to Question 86 addresses one of the perennial questions in the Christian tradition: If we are saved by grace, then why do good works? Why do we have to do anything? The succinct answer in the Catechism can be expressed in an even briefer form: You don't. You don't *have* to do anything. We live lives of faithfulness because we want to, because we are grateful. St. Augustine described the Christian life in these words: "Love God and do what you want."[4] That is, when we love God, our wants are transformed by the power of the Holy Spirit.

The theological and spiritual vision of grace and gratitude, central to our core identity, is an enduring legacy, worthy of our time and engagement. While institutional survival is not sufficient for our investment, seeing new and existing worshiping communities shaped by grace and gratitude is. We want to see communities shaped by grace and gratitude.

Stanley Hauerwas says that good theology does not necessarily lead us to good ethics but that bad theology eventually leads us to bad ethics. Gratitude sounds like a feeling where comfortable Presbyterians sit around and talk about how grateful they are for their stuff and how motivated they are to give away some of it. Gratitude is not fundamentally a feeling. It is a disposition; it is a profound thankfulness that is a response of faith to a God of grace.

If gratitude is the shape of our lives in response to a God of grace, then we can ask the question of what gratitude looks like in specific cases. We've thought a bit about what gratitude looks like in the context of polity: It looks like shared leadership for the sake of the gospel. There are so many crucial areas of ministry where we can ask these questions:

> What does gratitude look like in the context of structural racism?
>
> What does gratitude look like in the face of persistent sin?
>
> What does gratitude look like in the context of people living paycheck to paycheck?
>
> What does gratitude look like in the formation of children to follow Christ?
>
> What does gratitude look like in a world where some don't have clean water?
>
> What does gratitude look like in a context of government-sponsored violence?

Communities of Gratitude

One of the geniuses of the 1001 New Worshiping Communities initiative is that it embraces a nonlinear approach to the establishment of new worshiping communities. In the past, the effort would go into forming new congregations, and new congregations had a definite shape. Attempts to establish new congregations would begin in a predictable sequence: The first formal act of the community would be a worship service. After attracting a congregation to this worship service, the community would form, and eventually it would engage in formation around the Scriptures, would be involved in caring for one another, and eventually would reach out in mission. The 1001 initiative doesn't prescribe such a rigid sequence. A new community might begin by engaging in mission together or by gathering together around caregiving or Bible study. It might begin with a group of friends looking to extend to others their love for Jesus Christ, or it might begin with a group of strangers who come together around common commitments. Worshiping together might be the first act in the progression of this community or the last, or it might emerge somewhere in the process.

We find the phrase *communities of gratitude* helpful in describing this nonlinear development of the worshiping community. Because gratitude encompasses the entirety of the believer's life in response to a God of grace, it also encompasses the entirety of the community's life in response to a God of grace.

What does this gratitude in the community look like?

A Confessing Community. A people assured of God's grace in Christ is a community that is enabled to confess its sin. However, in the old model, we assumed that everyone knew they were sinful and that the job of the Christian community was to give them space to confess their sins and receive assurance of forgiveness. Worshiping communities now engage many people who don't think they're sinful and thus have no sense of their need for forgiveness. We need not panic, thinking that the gospel does not apply here. In an odd way, in this moment, part of our ministry is to teach people that they are indeed sinful. It may sound funny, but we offer people a gift when we help them learn that they are sinful and in need of forgiveness.

How so? John Calvin said that the knowledge of God and the knowledge of ourselves are intertwined. When we encounter the holy beauty of God, it is like a mirror being held up to us, and we see ourselves as both beautiful creations of God and as sinful people in need of forgiveness. And God is not surprised by this sin. Traditionally this happens in worship when we come into encounter with God and find the need to confess our sins. But we may also have this mirror put up before our eyes when we are involved in ministry to the homeless, or in building a community garden, or while talking with a friend over coffee.

A Faithful Community. As a forgiven community, one of the gifts of grace we receive is freedom. When we answer the question "If God saves you by grace, why do you have to do anything?" in terms of grace, we emphasize a deep and abiding freedom to the person who follows Christ. We rest in God's grace and are energized and satisfied with being faithful. We cannot be responsible for fixing the world. We can be free and dedicated to following Christ into the most difficult of situations, seeking to establish the kingdom of God.

A Peaceful Community. Paul greeted New Testament communities by saying, "Grace *and* peace be with you." The grace of our Lord Jesus Christ brings us peace with God and with one another. Few acts in worship, formal or informal, are as profound as passing the peace of Christ to one another.

I (Charles) didn't grow up with passing the peace, so I resisted actually saying, "The peace of Christ," to others in worship. It wasn't until my wife and I became part of Blacknall Memorial Presbyterian Church in Durham, North Carolina, that this movement of the service began to take root in my life. There I learned that this liturgical expression was the first act of gratitude, the first act of living reconciliation within the Christian community. Christ is our peace (Eph. 2:14).

Our gratitude for God's grace is intensely personal, yet it moves beyond the personal. God's grace is not limited to my needs or the needs of my congregation, for God loves the world. The Scriptures are clear about God's concern for the poor, God's desire for justice, God's mercy on the oppressed.

Our lives and our prayers should reflect these dual, related realities. Within a worshiping community, we need to be close enough to some that we can share our need for prayer in matters that are quite personal. And within a worshiping community, our prayers should attend to all those around the world who are in need. We need to pray about jobs and health—and for those who are hungry, are victims of violence, are addicted, are oppressed. We need to ask the question of our own complicity or even active engagement in systems that oppress others. Just as peace has been extended to us, we extend it to one another.

As we will see in a deeper way in the chapter on the missional character of new worshiping communities, communities of gratitude see their calling as focused on those outside the community, those whom God loves and desires to be drawn into the new realm of God. There is no doubt that a healthy community will practice mutual care, a bonding together as a community, a community bond of joy, but this internal strength becomes not a boundary to those outside it but an impetus to love them. The peace of Christ calls us to a missional life.

A Generous Community. Worshiping communities are formed around a God who loves out of pure grace, out of pure generosity. Thus worshiping communities reflect this generosity back toward God and one another. This is generosity in all its dimensions. Being generous with our judgments of each other may be one of the greatest gifts we can give one another. John Calvin wrote that we humans are unable to see what is truly in another person's heart, so we must treat one another with a generous judgment.

Generosity of time is one of the secrets to a true community—giving the time to become a true community instead of just an association of individuals. Overwhelmed by busyness in our own lives, we struggle with giving time to the people in our worshiping communities.

Speaking of a generosity of our possessions is always a bit tricky in Christian communities because many of us have been turned off by ministers and other Christian leaders who are always asking for money. We will look at this more closely in chapter 9, but our generosity involves our stuff, including our money. In a startling reflection on what it means to obey the commandment "Do not steal," the Westminster Larger Catechism gives a much broader meaning, including "giving and lending freely" and to "endeavor by all just and lawful means to procure, preserve, and further the wealth and outward estate of others."[5] This means that all that we have is from God and is to be used for God's purposes. The point of a generous life is not to support a worshiping community but to be a blessing to others with all that we have.

A Bold Community. One of the things we most dislike about common portrayals of Christians these days is that we just aren't that interesting, that we are a kind of bland yet judgmental people. A community of gratitude is a community that knows God is the one who holds all things, so we can be bold and creative and take risks because we don't have to figure everything out or ensure a particular outcome. One of the most profound sentences in the polity of the Presbyterian Church (U.S.A.) is that a worshiping community "is to be a community of faith, entrusting itself to God alone, even at the risk of losing its life."[6] Part of the DNA of new worshiping communities is that they are bold, risk-taking communities whose life together may last only a few years or might last for decades. Instead of trying to build long-term institutions, we hope to see creative, faithful communities whose witness isn't hampered by the need for institutional survival.

New Worshiping Communities as Communities of Gratitude. The vision of establishing 1001 New Worshiping Communities grows out of this assurance that the grace of the Lord Jesus Christ is with us, is for us, is for all. This presence of Jesus Christ is winsome, welcoming, transforming. It is a grace that comes to us just as we are but will not leave us as we are. It is a transforming grace. And all we can do in response is to express gratitude for the Spirit's presence in our life and in the life of the community.

1001 New Worshiping Communities is not a measurable goal to save a dying church or to rescue a denomination. If that is all it were, it would be a colossal waste of time. It is far more important than these pedestrian goals.

Because we believe that this is genuinely good news, we want to proclaim it, live it, celebrate it. It is this vision of a gracious God who comes to us in the person of Jesus Christ in the power of the Holy Spirit that draws from us a wholehearted grateful response. It is this vision that drives the 1001 New Worshiping Communities initiative.

2

NEW: *What's New in New Worshiping Communities?*

There has been no denying the energy and creativity unleashed by the movement of the 1001 initiative since its launch in 2012. Hundreds of new communities have hit the ground running, new baptisms abound, the ethnic and international diversity of the church has exploded, and the elusive millennial generation has turned out in droves. But there are some important questions to consider concerning the value of novelty and its relationship to the New Testament concept of transformation:

— How does innovation relate to the Holy Spirit's activity of transformation?
— Can we become something new without losing our identity and core purpose?

BACKGROUND

In the earliest days after the rollout of the initiative, PC(USA) leaders turned to the Fresh Expressions movement. Fresh Expressions emerged seven years previously from conversations among several denominations in the United Kingdom, including the Church of England. The movement catalyzed thousands of "fresh expressions of church" that looked very similar to our new worshiping communities in their incorporation of a missional theology and a contextual manifestation of church. The Fresh Expressions movement grew out of intentional reflection on the unique mission and current condition of the church along with deep sociological analysis of life in the UK around the turn of the millennium. The news was sobering, as recounted in a 2004 report from the Archbishop of Canterbury:

> Much of Britain's self-understanding comes from centuries of Christian faith, but many in Britain now have minimal knowledge of the Christian faith. The Christian story is no longer at the heart of the nation. Although people may identify themselves as "Christian" in the national census, for the majority that does not involve belonging to a worshipping community, or any inclination that it should. Many people have no identifiable religious interest or expression. Among some young people there is little evidence of any belief in a transcendent dimension. During the twentieth century Sunday school attendance dropped from 55 per cent to 4 per cent of children meaning that even the rudiments of the Christian story and of Christian experience are lacking in most young people.[1]

The report concluded, however, that the changes in the culture "present a moment of opportunity, a challenge to confidence in the gospel, and a call to imaginative mission."[2] The vision for Fresh Expressions arose from that milestone report. The term *fresh* was chosen because it echoed the word of the Anglican "Declaration of Assent," which ministers profess when they are licensed. However, the interpretation of the term in this new context sheds light on the word *new* as used in the PC(USA)'s *new worshiping communities*.

> The phrase **fresh expressions of church** is used in this report. The Preface to the Declaration of Assent, which Church of England ministers make at their licensing, states "The Church of England . . . professes the faith uniquely revealed in the Holy Scriptures and set forth in the catholic creeds, which faith the Church is called upon to proclaim afresh in each generation." The term "fresh expressions" echoes these words. It suggests something new or enlivened is happening, but also suggests connection to history and the developing story of God's work in the Church. The phrase also embraces two realities: existing churches that are seeking to renew or redirect what they already have, and others who are intentionally sending out planting groups to discover what will emerge when the gospel is immersed in the mission context.[3]

A denomination such as the Presbyterian Church (U.S.A.) that holds title to hundreds of aging, derelict buildings and where the average age of members is over sixty can certainly use a dose of *new*. However, the pursuit of novelty for its own sake can lead the church down a dead-end street and divert energy and resources from the church's mission.

WHAT DO WE MEAN BY NEW?

Steve Yamaguchi is dean of students and assistant professor of pastoral theology at Fuller Theological Seminary in Pasadena, California. Previously he served as executive presbyter in the Presbytery of Los Ranchos, California, where he helped to start and resource new worshiping communities over a period of several years. During that time, he appreciated the impact of new worshiping communities on the whole church. Steve provides helpful commentary on our use of the word *new*.

> We have operated with different notions of *new* for years. If I learn of a new McDonald's or Starbucks store, I have a clear idea of what to expect when I visit. There was a carefully prescribed formula and template for these "new" stores. These were not new creations or expressions of new creativity, but rather they were expressions of a model that had worked previously and was expected to work again.
>
> They were new in that they were new copies of an old model. For decades Presbyterians invested large sums of money in "new" church developments. It cost lots of money, and it counted on a prescribed model. The people who provided the money also provided the model. By the end of the last century Los Ranchos began facing the reality that that NCD model was neither viable nor sustainable. Many of the last of the so-called new church developments, built on anachronistic assumptions of the church's place in society, have struggled if they have survived at all. New reproductions were not manifesting new creation.
>
> The ready temptation in Los Ranchos in the face of the faltering new church reproduction model is often to shop for new models in an environment filled with a variety of sleek and shiny new products. Within the bounds of the presbytery were located the Crystal Cathedral, the mother church of Calvary Chapel, the mother ship of the Vineyard, Chuck Swindoll's Evangelical Free Church congregation, the TBN Broadcasting Network, Rick Warren's Saddleback Church, and dozens of lesser-known megachurches. In the midst of such a buffet of delights to the eye, some mainline churches and pastors

seemed to thrash around desperately for new ideas the way some mall shoppers hope they will look like and live the lifestyle of celebrities by wearing the designer outfits they sell. New for the sake of newness is not the kind of new that will serve us well. (Yamaguchi)

We live in a world that glorifies the new, the next, and the now. We stand in line for the latest fashions, eagerly await the state-of-the-art car designs, anticipate novelty in entertainment, restaurants, electronics, and toys. We hope to be constantly amazed by the latest and greatest new thing. One could begin to wonder if the new worshiping communities movement is just a theological twist on the cultural passion for novelty. Are we seeking new for the sake of newness? Are we bored or restless with our lives and looking for distraction? Do we bow to the idol of innovation? Can we really believe that God is changing with the times? That God adapts and adjusts to peculiarities of culture?

The kind of new that the 1001 New Worshiping Communities initiative hopes to usher in is the newness that comes from transformation—*metamorphóō*, which appears in the Epistles (Rom. 12:2; Cor. 3:18) to describe the newness accomplished by the Spirit of God. The same word shows up in Matthew 17:2 and Mark 9:2 to describe what the disciples witnessed at the transfiguration.

Metamorphosis in this New Testament sense is not becoming something essentially different, but it is about revealing another dimension of one's true nature. At the transfiguration, Jesus did not become more divine or glorious, but his intrinsic nature was revealed to the disciples in a new way. He did not become something novel, rather the disciples were able to see more clearly his real self.

To borrow from modern understandings of biology, even though the external and even the internal form may look dramatically different—almost unrecognizable—the DNA remains the same. The aversive, tree-destroying caterpillar metamorphoses into the beautiful, graceful pollenating butterfly. But its DNA is still the same; both come from the same egg and are both expressions of a single creature's life cycle. It seems that in our quest for what is new we must not forsake our DNA. Our history matters. Where we have come from matters. Those who have gone before matter. I become concerned when young leaders become zealous about their newly discovered ways of being church without any sense of connection to their church forebears. It reminds me of myself in the late 1960s and early '70s during the fervor of the Jesus Movement in Southern California. The way the

gospel was pitched to me, I actually believed that Jesus had been discovered (or maybe invented) somewhere around 1968. (Yamaguchi)

WE NEED BOTH

Michael Moynagh of Fresh Expressions has this helpful reminder:
"Ready-made answers from the past might be inadequate to cope with
new developments. . . . Innovation occurs as the Spirit contextualizes
the tradition to new situations. What steers this contextualization is
wisdom. Innovation is fundamental to the Christian inheritance."[4]

But the cult of novelty can be just as tempting and just as dangerous
as the cult of tradition. Both come from the same misconstruction: that
how we worship trumps who we worship. At a time of vast, discontinu-
ous change in the whole global culture, we can easily lose our moor-
ing if we cut our deep roots of faith. The foundation of the church is
and always has been the person of Jesus Christ. God is the eternal, the
alpha and omega, the same yesterday, today, and tomorrow. Yet God
is also the one who makes all things new, who brings forth new life and
new purpose. The Spirit of God has done marvelous works of spiritual
renewal and transformation throughout history and continues to work
in the world today.

Ken Baker, executive presbyter of the Presbytery of San Fernando,
sums this up: "The new worshiping communities challenge the traditional congregations to engage more intentionally in the world. And
the traditional congregations challenge the new worshiping communities to really lift up our reformed traditions. . . . We need both."[5]

TRANSFORMATION

These musings about newness set the stage for a wider conversation
about God's vision for resurrection and transformation in individual
lives, in the church, and in the world. New worshiping communities
reflect God's ongoing work of renewal in a hope-starved world. They
find their prototypes in the church of the first century instead of the
twentieth century. They draw on a rich history of disciple-making
and church planting while opening doors for new imagination for the
church of the twenty-first century. With gratitude to the God who,
deeply rooted in history, continues to transform lives and communities,

faithful followers today seek to engage in new expressions of the gospel. New worshiping communities are awakening the imagination of the faithful. Steve Yamaguchi encourages us to engage with the full, cosmic depth of newness.

> When we think of newness, I hope that we will capture the profound, cosmic wonder of what it means to be a "new creation" in Christ (2 Cor. 5:17). On the one hand, our newness is grounded in the ancient promises of God and in the continuity of God's faithfulness through all generations; thus we must remember our history. But we are also new creations, and there is another 2 Corinthians 5:17 sense in which everything old has passed away. This sense of being rescued from death and delivered to life is the compelling reality to which the church responds in gratitude, and then it joyfully proclaims this new life in Christ. In a nutshell, I am hoping that our focus on newness will capture this sense that in Christ life wins over death, that what is new is not simply an incremental improvement in religious expression but is an expression of the joy we have because the sweet aroma of life removes the stench of death. To lay all my cards on the table, my view of this is strongly shaped by my 12-step experience in the rooms and program of Alcoholics Anonymous, where I find some of the most joyful, thankful, inclusive, and life-giving communities I experience—far greater than what I have experienced in most Presbyterian churches thus far in my life. When we remember that everything is on the line and that the main question is life or death, then the gift of life in the face of imminent death has a way of focusing attention, resolve, and gratitude. I long for this zest and focus and joy to be known more and more, in newer and newer ways, in our PC(USA).
>
> I dearly hope for our new worshiping communities that what is new in this movement will not be mere novelty but will be a remembering of who and what we really are in Christ, that it will be the church metamorphosing—even at times being transfigured—to reveal to the world more and more of our true self as the vital, life-giving, faithful witness to the church's one Lord: Jesus Christ. (Yamaguchi)

3

New: Forming New Disciples

A NEW KIND OF QUESTION

"I'm not really a Christian, and I don't know if I'll ever be one. But I like it here, and I think something good is happening here. Is it all right with you if I get involved in this church if I'm not a Christian?"[1]

That question came from a young participant in the Hot Metal Bridge Faith Community on the South Side of Pittsburgh. It illustrates a feature of new worshiping communities everywhere: the participation of people who do not identify themselves as people of faith. What does that mean about profession of faith, church membership, and discipleship?

New worshiping communities "seek to make and form new disciples of Jesus Christ." Turning Methodists, Baptists, or Lutherans into Presbyterians; convincing faithful church members to ditch their own traditions to join the Presbyterian bandwagon; luring reluctant churchgoers from their pews with more enticing programs—those are not the ambitions of new worshiping communities. Those people matter and may well find their way into the life of a new worshiping community, but they are not the primary audience. People who have never had a relationship with God or who have drifted far away from church—those are the people new worshiping communities seek to engage in a fresh way.

This is a great time in history to do just that. A recent Gallup poll shows that church affiliation in the United States has steeply declined in the past decade, especially among the millennial generation. Yet over 90 percent of the U.S. population claims to believe in God.[2] In their book *Lost in America*, Tom Clegg and Warren Bird have this to say: "The unchurched population in the United States is so extensive that, if it were a nation, it would be the fifth most populated nation on the planet."[3] The harvest is plentiful, as Jesus proclaims in Luke 10:2. Disciple-making is the calling of the church, and the time to fulfill that calling is now.

DOUBTERS AND DISCIPLES

One circumstance common to new worshiping communities that confounds members of traditional churches is the deep engagement of people who do not identify themselves as followers of Jesus. The Table in Casper, Wyoming, announces itself as a place for "doubters and disciples together." The Hot Metal Bridge Faith Community sponsors Bible Fight Club, where people passionately engage Scripture with all their questions, doubts, and complaints right on the table. The Adirondack Church Without Walls organizes hikes and rafting trips for believers and nonbelievers that include stops to reflect on the glory of creation and the nature of the Creator. The Arabic Presbyterian Fellowship in Huntington Beach, California, has developed a partnership with Muslims who had been their enemies in their native Egypt.

There are communities where people from other faiths or of no faith participate because they find belonging and a shared commitment to justice. Meanwhile, members of established churches mostly worship beside others who share their beliefs and traditions.

NEW DISCIPLES

The language in the definition of new worshiping community speaks of making new *disciples* in contrast to making new *converts*. The process of disciple-making assumes a relationship that is built over a period of time through mutual interests and shared time. Disciple-making involves humility, listening, and friendship. The image many carry of conversion, whether based on reality or not, involves knocking on the doors of strangers and asking if they have been saved. If they answer in the negative, the next step is to frighten them into salvation and then move on to the next house. This caricature has become so imprinted on the minds of people in our culture that it has frightened many away from any involvement with self-professed Christians.

Ironically, it might be that the work of evangelism is actually getting in the way of the work of disciple-making. Are we trading in the opportunity for a lifelong journey of spiritual discovery with a fellow traveler for the promise of a quick fix? Are we scaring away the very people God has provided as our companions along the way?

Author Madeline L'Engle explains the paradox this way: "We draw people to Christ not by loudly discrediting what they believe, by telling them how wrong they are and how right we are, but by showing them a light that is so lovely that they want with all their hearts to know the source of it."[4]

BUILDING COMMUNITY TAKES TIME

A new generation of missional church planters seeks to find ways of becoming part of a community, building trust through mutual friendship based on true affection, not on ulterior motive, and then pointing people toward that lovely light. This kind of disciple-making can be a long process, requiring a commitment of time and presence over years. This is not the fast-food version of religion. For this reason, the new worshiping communities of the twenty-first century tend to grow slowly, and many retain a small, familylike feeling. The median size of new worshiping communities is thirty-three persons, reflecting the desire for intimacy and authenticity in relationships.[5]

The phenomenon of people within Presbyterian new worshiping communities who do not self-profess as followers of Jesus worries critics of the movement. Traditionally, a profession of faith or confirmation of baptism has been considered the entry price into the church community. What are we to make of faith communities that include people who do not share in professing faith, who are openly struggling with or even resisting the embrace of Christianity?

A NEW WAY OF THINKING ABOUT DISCIPLESHIP

Cynthia L. Rigby, professor of theology at Austin Presbyterian Theological Seminary, has some compelling ideas about what it means to form new disciples in the church of the twenty-first century that are based on Karl Barth's analysis of the story of Jesus' crucifixion along-side two criminals. Her reflections challenge common assumptions about discipleship and about this well-known biblical story. We feel comfortable embracing the "good" criminal as a disciple, even holding up his end-of-life confession as a marker of hope. But what about the criminal who rails against Jesus from the cross? Surely, he can't also be a disciple, can he?

> I have lately been pondering a sermon by Karl Barth titled, "The Criminals with Him."[6] In this sermon (on Luke 23:33), Barth makes what might seem to be a startling claim, even to those of us with Reformed sensibilities. He says that when the dying Jesus promises, "Today you will be with me in Paradise," he is making this promise not only to the criminal who respects and advocates for him but also to the one who derides and seemingly rejects him. Barth goes on to identify the three who die together on the cross as "the first Christian community." Even before the twelve disciples of Jesus are part of the community of faith, Barth insists, the criminals have been ushered in, by the grace of God.
>
> Barth's interpretation of this text is unusual, but it is consistent with Reformed theological emphases. Most interpreters of all theological persuasions recognize that Jesus is acting graciously toward the criminal who defends him without entertaining the possibility that the derisive criminal might also be included in the promise. But we Reformed Christians do not believe we have any role in accomplishing our own salvation, including by way of our own acknowledgment of or dismissal of God's grace. It is not that what we believe or don't believe doesn't matter, we hold, but that what we believe or don't believe has absolutely no bearing on the fact of God's claim on us. Whatever the criminals' differences are in responding to Jesus, they are not indicative of whether or not they are heirs to the promise of paradise. (Rigby)

BEGIN WITH BELONGING

One of the gifts that new worshiping communities offer to the wider church is a close association between believers and nonbelievers. Author Diana Butler Bass has this to say: "Christianity did not begin with a confession. It began with an invitation into friendship, into creating a new community, into forming relationships based on love and service."[7]

The missional leaders called to start new worshiping communities enter a neighborhood with the intention of listening and learning about that neighborhood from those who are already invested in the well-being of the neighborhood. They spend time in restaurants, libraries, gyms, basketball courts, schools, and knitting shops, connecting with people and the activities that engage the people of the neighborhood. It is out of these relationships that community grows. People who feel lonely or isolated or who are seeking purpose or meaning in their lives find, in a new worshiping community, a place that seems to offer something—fellowship, warmth, invitation, purpose, service—that connects with their perceived need. Belonging just makes sense.

Bass has been frequently quoted in her assumption that the traditional pathway toward discipleship can be summarized as "believe, behave, belong," the assumption being that first one understands and gives assent to the basic tenets of faith. This often comes through a confirmation class, the study of a catechism, or years of faithful Sunday school attendance. After showing some grasp of the doctrines, the new believer assumes the practices of the community: serving others, giving tithes, engaging in the life of the church, learning the habits and behaviors that accompany the doctrine. Finally, after demonstrating the expected moral codes and lifestyle, the confirmand goes through a ritual of belonging—baptism or public affirmation of faith—and officially becomes a member. No wonder so many teenagers speak of their confirmation as their "graduation." It feels more like the culmination of the journey than the beginning.

Bass questions whether this process correctly reflects the trajectory of discipleship in today's church. She offers up a new suggestion: that the journey begins with belonging to a welcoming community where the journeyer is embraced. Within the safety of this acceptance, the person observes rhythms of behavior that shape the community and begins to participate in the rhythms that may include prayer, Sabbath-keeping, worship, service, silence, and study. Being in proximity with other disciples and acting in the same way as they do, engaging in conversations along the way, may lead to the desire to go deeper. Giving intellectual assent to the premises that lie behind the actions may be a much later development. She suggests that a more accurate description of the pattern is belong, behave, believe.

If that is so, the "bad" criminal on the cross has jumped right into the activity of discipleship, bypassing the introductory instruction, by dying along with Jesus. Where, then, on that trajectory does discipleship happen?

> A closer look at the role of the derisive criminal in the story may not reveal a person growing in gratitude for what he is witnessing. But it does show a genuine participation in the event of Christ's suffering and death. . . . Notice that the criminal demonstrates he is "with" Jesus in more than only a literal sense. In speaking so scornfully to and about him, the criminal shows he understands himself to be in relationship to Jesus, even if he frames that relationship as hostile.
>
> While I don't think the derisive criminal's hostile daring of Jesus "accomplishes" discipleship, I do think it is a manifestation of the Spirit's work in and through the criminal, drawing him to participation in the event of Christ. I think the same about the other criminals' confession and request. Again, it is not that the affirming criminal has the "right" response to Jesus, and therefore shows himself a true disciple, while the derisive criminal rejects discipleship. It is, rather, that each is graced with the capacity to be with the Jesus who is with them, though granted in very different ways. (Rigby)

Rigby urges us to broaden our understanding of how "participating in Christ" might be a first step in the journey of discipleship in new worshiping communities. The public confession we have traditionally expected as the starting point for a life of faith may not be the only (or even the most common) entry to the journey of discipleship.

> We associate disciples almost solely with those who make public confessions of faith, with those willing to say what they believe, with those willing to stand with the community of faith and join in to the great confessions of our church. My exploration here seems a bit radical even to me, but it is this: to reflect on whether we might recognize as disciples not only those who believe and confess but those who disbelieve and struggle to confess, not only those who have "firm and certain knowledge of God's benevolence toward us,"[8] but also those who are skeptical, for example, that God is benevolent, given the sufferings of the world. . . . I am suggesting that we include in our circle of disciples not only believers who doubt, but those who want to believe but are unable to set their skepticism to the side in order to make the leap into faith. The question for us is this: Are we ready and willing to join in fellowship with those who (like the derisive criminal

on the cross) are deeply skeptical that the lofty promises of God will
be kept, given the circumstances in which we find ourselves? (Rigby)

Rigby wonders if the church might gain new appreciation of the
"nones" in contemporary society by expanding what might be appropriate responses to God's promises. As we suggested in chapter 2, gratitude is not confined to a kind of bourgeois thankfulness. She suggests
incredulity, doubt, and skepticism to be among other possible faithful
ways of responding to the grace of God.

> When we recognize disciples who have a full range of responses to
> the gospel but are still participating in it in one way or another, we
> will be better positioned to see what new worshiping communities
> already look like and to imagine how else they might look. These
> communities, unlike ours, might not place gratitude at the center of
> their worship, as we do. But their expressions of lament and praise, of
> doubt and faith; their questioning interpretations of Scripture; their
> righteous anger at the ways in which Christian communities through
> the ages have perpetuated the status quo will, I would hope, open
> up what God promises us in fresh, honest, and "on the ground" ways.
>   I think we might begin by recognizing that there are more dis-
> ciples in our midst—in our churches and in our culture at large—than
> we may be aware. The "nones," for example, are not atheists and may
> or may not identify as "seekers." Many of them are deeply skeptical
> about the claims of the Christian faith, and they often can articulate
> good reasons why. They are not interested in becoming members
> of religious institutions, but this does not mean they are unable to
> make commitments. . . . How do we reach out to fellow disciples who
> are telling us they have no interest in participating in Christian com-
> munities as we know them and appreciate them? A start might be to
> recognize them as disciples to begin with, and be genuinely inter-
> ested in learning from them instead of being eager only to facilitate
> their "Christian formation"—as if we are somehow more spiritually
> advanced. (Rigby)

If expansion of our definition of discipleship is a first step in our goal
of disciple-making, where might we go from there as we seek to form
new worshiping communities in a rapidly changing context? Rigby
suggests that the mysteries of faith might provide an appealing access
point to unchurched people.

A next step might be to invite them to transfigurations. To awe. To the mystery that is participation in Christ. We might invite them, no strings attached or even *apparently* attached, to the Lord's Table. . . . This is because it is precisely at the Table that we, like the derisive criminal, enter concretely into the life, death, and resurrection of Jesus Christ. It is at the Table that we are closest to the criminals who are closest to him, sharing in the shedding of blood. The bread and the cup function, then, as a means of grace. Our discipleship and our discipling both need more of these mystical experiences tied to our metaphysical convictions—Table as well as Word, of course; the two are inextricably intertwined, as they were on the cross. . . . Whatever else we hope to achieve in the kingdom is never going to happen if we fail to integrate discipleship and disciple-making into the heart of our practices. If we fail in discipleship, the whole thing fails. (Rigby)

THE MISSION FIELD

New worshiping communities grapple with the challenge of recognizing that the mission field is right outside the doors of the church, in the communities and neighborhoods around us. They recognize a hunger for meaning and purpose in all humanity and seek to build relationships and create situations where the experience of God happens, especially in the hearts of unchurched people.

In fact, this fresh understanding of discipleship starts to sound a whole lot like the relationship Jesus had with the original disciples. There was a group who participated in kingdom-building work without demonstrating a whole lot of mature theological understanding of the mission they were engaged in. Their "professions of faith" were intermittent and impulsive.

Jesus has got a whole lot of "preconversion disciples" tagging along with him. All the while, he's just discipling them along the way until the gospel narrative finally weaves its way into their hearts and they come alive to God in new birth. They're certainly not mature, born-again Christians. What is even more surprising is that they are actually involved in his ministry even before they are fully converted to Jesus and his mission. (Rigby)

Like the original twelve, today's disciples may find their way into participation in God's mission—with the homeless, in disaster response, in hunger alleviation, in protest against injustice, in welcoming refugees, in caring for the elderly—long before they can or are willing to articulate a profession of faith. At the heart of new worshiping communities is a recognition that there is more to discipleship than a single moment of conversion. Discipleship involves a lifelong journey of taking on the practices of the beloved community. Living in a quick-fix society, we find it tempting to seek easy answers to life's deepest challenges. What if, instead, the church embraced discipleship as a "long obedience in the same direction," to use Eugene Peterson's formulation?[9] What if lament and doubt and anger and questions were part of the journey instead of the baggage we leave behind when we choose to follow Christ?

HOLY SPIRIT WORK

For many decades, the Presbyterian Church and most other mainline denominations believed that starting new churches was a matter of putting up new buildings with state-of-the-art facilities that would entice people with their attractive programs. In an increasingly non-Christian culture, the "If we build it, they will come" approach to church planting disappoints church people again and again, leaving behind a trail of debt and discouragement.

Making new disciples through the power of the Holy Spirit, on the other hand, happens best through one-on-one or small group relationships. It requires no expensive building or carefully crafted programs. It demands that mature Christians leave behind the conceit that they know all the answers and learn to listen to others. It involves trust in the Holy Spirit and belief that God is already at work in the harvest field making disciples. It involves starting off on a journey alongside fellow travelers, guided by the Holy Spirit without a preconceived vision of where the path may lead.

4

New: Forms of Church

Despite the old Sunday school song about how the church is not a building, most people continue to hold fast to the idea that a church belongs to a particular address. A church without real estate feels insubstantial. Yet new worshiping communities flourish in libraries, gyms, coffee shops, parks, and living rooms. Some use the whole neighborhood as their parish. Can a nomadic community be a real church? Is eleven o'clock on Sunday morning a sacred hour? Do we need to have a seminary-trained, ordained minister in the pulpit? Do we even need a pulpit? What are the absolute essentials of church? How do we explore new forms of church for a changing culture? These are questions at the heart of the 1001 New Worshiping Communities initiative. They are questions about ecclesiology. They are important inquiries about what we mean by *church* and about what the 1001 initiative contributes to the conversation about the changing face of the church in the twenty-first century.

In this chapter, we draw on the work of two theologians who discuss the meaning of church, factors of contemporary culture that shape our understanding of church, and how saints of the past have addressed cultural shifts, for better or for worse. Christopher James is assistant professor of evangelism and missional Christianity at the University of Dubuque Theological Seminary, and Scott Hagley is assistant professor of missiology at Pittsburgh Theological Seminary.

COMMUNITY VERSUS CHURCH

The term *new worshiping community* intentionally avoids the word *church*. Many people have questioned this decision. Are we rejecting the history, tradition, and theology that come with the word *church?* Why do we need to invent new language? In exploring the definition, one can hardly avoid bumping into a solid, intentional ecclesiology. Why the need for a smokescreen?

For most of the history of Protestantism in North America, new churches have begun with a building. In an 1870 report to the General Assembly, the Joint Committee on Church Erection states, "The Church edifice is the material nucleus around which the spiritual elements gather and take their permanent shape. If any comparison can be made, it is more important to secure the church . . . than it is to secure the missionary himself. We may provide the missionary next year, but with land for a Church it is now or never."[1]

As we noted earlier, the formula for starting a new church has insisted on the following steps: buy a piece of property, erect a building, conduct a nationwide search for an experienced pastor and staff, conduct a massive advertising campaign, and launch a worship service with all the components in place. Replacing the organ with a praise band, hymnals with projection screens, and pews with theater seats have been attempts to make the worship service more "culturally relevant." In the twentieth century, this formula for new church development resulted in massively expensive projects that were difficult to sustain except in affluent communities. Most ecclesiastical councils can point to at least one instance where a new church building created such financial hardships as to make the judicatory wary of trying again. Church planting became a model for affluent, primarily white, suburbia. *Church*, in the minds of most people, meant building, staff, and Sunday morning worship.

STARTING WITH WORSHIP

The first way to connect with the new community has traditionally been through a service of worship, actually called a *launch*.

> Traditionally, new churches have sought to connect with new people by adapting their worship services to appeal to local culture and

tastes. This approach is still effective in some contexts with some people. However, as the population of those willing to attend a worship service as a first step in their spiritual journey shrinks and the number of those who are unchurched, unaffiliated, and uninterested rises, it is time to recognize that worship services, no matter how we redesign them, will not suffice as the assumed entry point into the life of the church. For the burgeoning number of Americans not raised in churches, or whose negative church experiences have derailed their faith, the journey to participation in church is increasingly likely to begin in experiences of authentic community or participating with Christians in serving those in need. As a result, it is critical that missional pioneers limit the amount of time they devote to crafting Word-and-sacrament gatherings so that they are able to actively experiment with ways in which the core ecclesial practices of worship, fellowship, and mission might open out into environments in which outsiders can experience real community, serve the common good, and engage in spiritual exploration. (James)

THE CHURCH IS NOT A BUILDING

Subtracting the assumption of owning a building from the plan opens the door to fresh ideas about the form of church. For certain individuals, the church building itself carries unwanted baggage. Stained-glass windows and organ music may convey disagreeable memories or may simply feel intimidating to someone who has never crossed the threshold of a church building. A stool at their favorite bar, a park bench, or a seat at a friend's dinner table may feel more inviting.

The term *new worshiping community* has opened the imagination of many. It freed visionaries who hesitated to take on the responsibility for maintaining a building, sustaining a staff, or launching a program to try something brand new. Young adults and new immigrant groups especially responded to the idea of planting a community instead of a church. In a world that is increasingly compartmentalized and divided, a deep yearning for community emerges, even among those who would not identify as religious people.

My husband and I (Vera) attend a little brick church with a white steeple that is over 250 years old. The church is surrounded by a cemetery where Revolutionary War veterans rest under ancient oak trees.

We gather in pews at 9:30 every Sunday morning, listen to organ music, enjoy the sun shining through antique stained-glass windows, and always recite the Apostles' Creed. And we are perfectly happy with our church experience. This doesn't mean that it is the right context for the Bhutanese refugees who have moved into our neighborhood and who speak little English. Nor is it necessarily the right environment for our twenty-two-year-old son who seldom sees 9:30 on a Sunday morning.

NEW FORMS OF CHURCH

The 1001 initiative explores new forms of church, taking elements from ancient and modern expressions of church. Labyrinths, liturgy, incense, icons, and chants are as common in new worshiping communities as punk rock music, yoga, or a barista. New worshiping communities take clues from their local context to discern the form of worship that is appropriate to their participants, although they seldom begin with worship. Building relationships comes first—relationships with God and with neighbors. Out of those rich, nurturing relationships comes a vision for a contextual worship experience. The people of the community have a role in helping to shape the forms of worship, disciple-making, community outreach, and program that are meaningful to the context.

Scott Hagley reflects on the cultural changes that impact the church today and how they cause us to redefine the form of church for a changing world. Using the familiar metaphor of wine and wineskins, he points us toward an understanding of context as a prelude to focus on form.

> Jesus taught that new wine requires new wineskins. While this may be a dated metaphor, we tend to be drawn to the idea. Rapid cultural change and diminishing Christian social influence—called post-Christendom by some—has fixed our attention on strategic and organizational proposals for our "new missional era." We can choose between new "centered-set" or "apostolic" structures,[2] niche-group ministries or "simple" church,[3] outwardly focused church or new monasticism.[4] While these proposals have merit, our rush to the structural and strategic often obscures the deeply theological, imaginative, and contextual work that generates such forms. In our enthusiasm for the new wineskin, we forget the wine.

This affinity for the simply strategic is a temptation for new worshiping communities:

> The 1001 New Worshiping Communities initiative faces this same problem. As persons and congregations respond to the voice of the Holy Spirit and join the mission of God in the neighborhood, they will discover "new forms of church for changing cultural contexts."[5] But this discovery of new contextual expressions of church cannot be an end in itself. The new wineskins emerge in response to the new wine. When Christian communities act in hope, when we practice our faith in the gospel in the places God has sent us, we cultivate possibilities for new, contextual forms of church life to emerge.
>
> New forms for new worshiping communities originate with the open, hopeful postures of mission. . . . The community of Christ expects God to lead and attends to their experiences and challenges accordingly. They not only wait for "power from on high," but they also recognize and receive the gifts God grants for mission (Luke 24:49). New worshiping communities gather in homes or public spaces, welcome strangers, listen, and serve neighbors in expectant hope that the God who sends will also equip and empower in the Holy Spirit. The life of such a community begins when we actively participate in God's mission while we wait and discern God's Spirit. We act and also remain open to receive. We initiate and also respond. Flexible, mission-shaped structures emerge from attentive and receptive postures within a worshiping community's gathered and sent life. New worshiping communities discover church forms by walking in the way opened up by Jesus. New forms follow mission in hope.[6] (Hagley)

Hope is the key practice that helps new structures to emerge from an orientation toward what God is doing, when we anticipate the one who makes all things new.

Beginning with a focus on the *form* of church can lead us down an unproductive path. We often receive phone calls from people asking if we think it would be a good idea for them to start a coffee-shop church or to add a rock band to their worship service. We explain that we can't know the answer to their questions without becoming intimately aware of their context. Each of these could be good ideas or precisely the wrong way to engage a particular group. Hagley has another helpful comment:

> Our false starts in the search for missionary structures come when we quickly build structures in response to certain stimuli rather than

framing hope-filled anticipatory practices within particular contexts. We rush to create new wineskins, but forget that they are to hold the new wine of the gospel. Structure will follow mission, and mission is practiced hope. The practice of the church *does not* take its cue from the world, nor from concern for its own survival. It takes its cue from God's promised future. In our table fellowship, our hospitality, our spiritual disciplines, our shared concern for the neighborhood, . . . in the ways we order our lives together, we do so in hope, in anticipation of God's future. Let us remember the wine, and, as we share it, attend to the new forms of life that emerge. (Hagley)

MISSIONAL HOSPITALITY

Many leaders of new worshiping communities do a great job of moving into a neighborhood and building meaningful relationships. Some are especially gifted in individual disciple-making. But there comes a point where regular rhythms of worship are needed as the community matures. Chris James offers some helpful insights about how a particular community's worship can give meaning and purpose to the community and reflect God's faithfulness.

The church-planting team—as the nucleus of the new church—ought to form its life together in love for God, one another, and the world in regular rhythms of worship, fellowship, and mission, enriched by the full range of ecclesial activities including Word and sacrament. . . . Moreover, they ought to hope and pray that others will join them in this way of life, for it is this community of practice that is church in the fullest sense. It is with this love-filled hope that they set themselves to the task of discerning how they might foster space for others to draw near enough to see what the gospel looks like when it is embodied in the life of a community of disciples.

The initial core group begins to shape the new community as they meet and pray together and plan.

The concrete ways a core team might offer opportunities for spiritual exploration, community, and service are truly limitless. How they choose to engage in the space-making of missional hospitality is a matter for serious contextual, spiritual, and communal discernment. All are ways that contemporary disciples of Jesus in the U.S.

context are expressing their shared love for God, one another, and the world. As such, they are authentic forms of Christian worship, fellowship, and mission and instances of church being church. At the same time, they are examples of missional hospitality, because they create spaces in which church outsiders can participate fully without ascribing to Christian doctrine, stepping inside a Christian building, or affiliating with a Christian institution. These spaces allow people to belong (or serve, or explore spirituality) before they believe.

This provision of space for people to engage in the community is more than a strategy to get them in the door. It provides a profound and risky means for them to observe how the community is responding to God.

In addition, missional hospitality fosters environments in which non-Christians can observe the people of the church being church, engaging in their core ecclesial practices. They can not only observe the church serving but—by God's grace—begin to see that followers of Jesus serve as part of a larger mission to join God in the renewal of all things. And they may begin to notice the love that animates their mission as an echo of God's love for the world. They may not only see the church creating a community of friends but also catch glimpses of Christian fellowship as it offers a foretaste of the new redeemed humanity. They may not only see the church hosting conversations and experiences in spirituality but also begin to grasp what it means to worship God through Christ as a way of life. Missional hospitality makes room for our post-Christian neighbors to observe church being church.

While church will always reflect essential relationships with God, one another, and the world and will strive to express these in worship, fellowship, and mission, the new forms of church needed in our rapidly changing context will go further to form their ecclesial life and rhythms in ways that prioritize spaces of missional hospitality. (James)

RELATIONSHIPS COME FIRST

Exploring new forms of church for a changing culture is one of the goals of the 1001 initiative. As our country and world become increasingly pluralistic, it is clear that a one-size-fits-all model for church will not be adequate for church planting. On the other hand, there is a temptation to jump immediately to find the most creative, trendy, or shocking way to reimagine church. Examples like Serious Ju-Ju, a ministry in a skateboard park, or Adirondack Church Without Walls, an outdoor adventure ministry, will seem compelling and replicable. There is a temptation to rush into trying out new forms before engaging in the much harder work of building relationships, becoming part of a community, finding the people of peace in the neighborhood, and sharing spiritual stories.

For contextual church planting to have integrity, the relationships come first. In the words of church planter Corey Widmer, "We never meant to start a church. The mission came first, the relationships, the neighborhood came first. The pastors, the worship service, the institution—we just sort of threw all that stuff together at the end."[7]

In the 1001 movement, there will be at least 1001 different forms of church. They will have much to teach the wider church. Some may last for decades while others may have only temporary appeal. The key principle is that new worshiping communities begin by building life-giving, transformative relationships with people out of which the form of church emerges organically as new disciples take responsibility for worship in context.

5

WORSHIPING

What do we call these things? That was the question from the very beginning of this movement. And almost all the discussion was about the middle term. Everyone agreed on *new*. And everyone agreed on *communities*. The middle term, not so much. Were these new *worshiping* communities, new *missional* communities, new *witnessing* communities, *fresh expressions* of church, or something else? This disagreement on description revealed substantive disagreements about the purpose of these new communities.

Sometimes such disagreements can feel like the proverbial arguments over the number of angels who can dance on the head of a pin. However, as Stanley Hauerwas often says, "Description is everything." How one describes an ethical issue, how one describes the alternatives, has the answer embedded from the beginning. *Worshiping, missional, witnessing,* or *fresh expressions of church* are more than somewhat arbitrary descriptions of a movement—they point the movement in a particular direction.

This question is made more profound by two important contexts. One is post-Christendom. The end of Christendom, the decline of the white mainline church in North America, the growth of Pentecostalism, the rise of the nondenominational megachurch, and the return of Protestants to the Roman Church all highlight fundamental questions that those in the church are asking about the nature and purpose of the church.

The second important context is our need for shorthand references. Even if we grant that these new communities can have many dimensions to their life, at some point we need to find a shorthand terminology. The term *church* is loaded with expectation, and so we have these varieties of terms. And each such reference—*worshiping, missional, witnessing, fresh expressions*—privileges some aspect of the nature and purpose of the communities.

In particular, in the Presbyterian Church (U.S.A.), the phrase *new worshiping communities* was questioned by some because they believed it communicated that the primary activity of these new communities was gathering for weekly worship services and therefore the primary act of evangelism was inviting others to these worship services. The concern was that *worshiping* might perpetuate the "If you build it, they will come" model of church that flourished during Christendom.

As we work through these issues, we will do so with the guidance of two theologians: Darrell Guder, professor of missional and ecumenical theology emeritus at Princeton Theological Seminary, who is a winsome and deep proponent of missional theology; and Edwin van Driel, associate professor of theology at Pittsburgh Theological Seminary, who believes that the missional movement needs clarification to be more helpful.

THE MISSIONAL CHALLENGE

Missional has proven to be the most energizing term in Protestant ecclesiology over the past generation. Emerging out of the South African church's struggle to deal with the social systems of the apartheid era and given depth and breadth by Darrell Guder and others, the missional vision has captivated many.

For Guder, the missional movement is an effort to restore the contemporary church to the apostolic character of the early church: "The early Christian communities understood and experienced their gathered worship as missional formation. They knew themselves to be first and foremost apostolic communities, that is, communities called forth and empowered by God's Holy Spirit to continue the apostolic witness." This character of those early communities grew out of divine encounter: "Because of their encounter with the risen Christ and their empowered response to his claims upon them, they were

missionary by their very nature. To know Christ was to be his witness. To be his disciple meant to become his apostle. Their sense of
themselves was that they were to be light, leaven, and salt, as a minority movement on the margins of their social and cultural world."[1] In
short, the missional movement is an effort to help the church recover
its missionary vocation.

For Guder, this missional conversation is vital because the church
has limited and reduced the gospel by divorcing the evangelistic task
of announcing salvation from the missional task of calling, forming,
and sending particular Christian communities to witness to this salvation. This essentially malforms the community-centered character of
our calling so that it is focused on individual salvation. The missional
movement is an attempt, in great part, to reintegrate the individual and
corporate dimensions of the gospel.[2]

This integration is displayed for us in the New Testament texts
where we see that the calling of the community is *apostolic*. The first
Christians saw themselves as concrete embodiments of the ongoing
Spirit-empowered witness of the apostles. Their encounters with the
risen Christ were transformational—within themselves, in their associations, in their primary communities, in everything. There was no
division between knowing Christ or being saved by Christ and being a
witness to Christ.

This missionary character is reflected in what worship was eventually called. While the term *mass* has many associations for modern
Christians, most do not associate it with missionary sending. But *mass*
derives from the same Latin word from which we get *mission*: "Its root
meaning was 'sending,' and it was associated with the liturgical dismissal, which emphasized in the early rites that the faithful were now
being sent back into the world as God's servants and Christ's witnesses.
'In [the mass] is kindled the light which is to illuminate the world.'"[3]
But over time, this sending identity of those gathered in worship
degenerated and was shoved aside in favor of a preoccupation with the
salvation of its own members—and lest we believe this to be a medieval
Catholic error, Guder emphasizes that there was little change in this
regard in the Reformation.[4]

This emphasis on *sentness* as the core vocation of the church is in
tension with the most visible act of most Christian communities: gathering for worship. If being sent is the core vocation, why gather at all?
Guder believes that the sending shapes the gathering: "Every dimension

of Christian worship, every component of liturgy, must necessarily relate to the missional vocation of the church. The task of those who plan and lead the church's liturgical worship is missiological. It has to do with the intentional confession and celebration of the very nature of the church as a missionary people."[5]

The marks of the church, Word and sacrament, thus serve this vision of worship—they "work together to call and form the church as a missionary people."[6] Baptism is a sign of the washing away of sin, of inclusion in the Christian community, and of a vocational call: "After he rose from the dead, Jesus commissioned his followers to go and make disciples, baptizing them and teaching them to obey his commands. The disciples were empowered by the outpouring of the Spirit to continue Jesus' mission and ministry, inviting others to join this new way of life in Christ." These words of institution of the Lord's Supper speak of proclamation as well as remembrance. All of worship is a form of prayer: "Faithful prayer is shaped by God's Word in Scripture and inspires us to join God's work in the world."[7] As Guder believes, "Christian worship is, before the completion of the eschaton, not an end in itself, but an instrument for God's mission in the world. We are gathered in order to be sent."[8]

Many congregations take this new language and apply it to their current efforts in doing mission. *Missional* is not a neologism to describe what we already do, but is, for Guder, a challenge to the church's basic identity and orientation in the world. *Missional* describes the overarching orientation of the community that understands and acts as fundamentally called by God for the sake of the world. Even self-interested communities whose primary goal is the salvation of its own members can try to do something for those outside once in a while. It is the difference between an identity and an irregular, discrete task.

Charles has known Darrell Guder for a long time, and since the introduction of the 1001 New Worshiping Communities initiative, they have had some playful banter over the use of the term *worshiping*. Put simply, Guder is afraid that using *worshiping* as the primary descriptor of *communities* can lead to a reinforcement of the notion that the community exists primarily for its own members' benefit. For Guder, this is a matter of deep conviction.

> [It is] even if unintentionally so, a move away from the missiocentricity that is the apostolic focus which shapes the early church and the scriptures that are empowered to continue their formation. . . . There

are several missional reasons for this critique. The first is biblical. I have already alluded to this: the purpose of the apostolic mission was the formation of witnessing communities. That purpose shapes the scriptural testimony in such a way that a missional hermeneutic is essential to our engagement with the formative power of the Bible. . . .

We need to address anew the theological challenges of the linkage between the gathered life of the community and its scattered life in the world, the theology and practice of the sacraments as events of apostolic equipping for witness, the translation of the gospel into the languages and cultures into which we are sent, and the public witness of the corporate life of the community. At the heart of this endeavor must be the gathered life of the worshiping community. It is the center of the missional wheel from which the spokes move out into every aspect and dimension of the church's life in the world. (Guder)

A FRIENDLY CHALLENGE TO THE MISSIONAL MOVEMENT

Darrell Guder's incisive work on the missional character of the church has formed a new conversation about the church, one engaged by folks all over the world. For many, it has become the starting point. Edwin van Driel begins his theological work on new worshiping communities from this missional beginning: "Since the second half of the last century the church has rediscovered the centrality of 'mission' to the church's very existence. Mission is not one among many activities of the church; the church is, at its very core, missional." The church's life is embedded in the larger narrative of God's mission through the work of Jesus Christ to "gather and knit together the scattered fragments of humanity by drawing them out from under the authority of the powers that have governed them so far." The church is not simply instrumental in this gathering, it is "the visible result of this gathering activity, and its very existence bears witness to the powers that their time is up" (van Driel).

However, for many of us who find the basic missional argument convincing, questions remain. Put simply, the missional argument skews toward considering the making of a Christian people, the community, instrumental to mission. Van Driel argues that the community is sent *by* being gathered. This fine theological distinction needs some unpacking.

Van Driel relies on Ephesians and the rich description of the Christian community there in chapters 1 and 2. The overriding image of these chapters is of all things being gathered up in Jesus Christ (1:10). This gathering brings together "strangers to the covenants of promise" (2:12) who become "citizens with the saints and also members of the household of God" (2:19). Now Jew and Gentile alike can be knit together in a new humanity (2:21). Van Driel argues that this description is the goal of God's "plan for the fullness of time" (1:10) that began before the foundation of the world (1:4). Van Driel strikes against an instrumental view of the community: "In other words, to be gathered into this new community, this new household of God, is not accidental to who we are, but it is our eschatological destiny. It is that for which we were created" (van Driel).

While Guder can be read to say that we gather in order to be sent, van Driel suggests that the gathering work is itself salvific. We don't gather and then somehow acquire salvation, but being gathered into the new community constitutes salvation. Salvation in this sense goes beyond forgiveness of sins to mean participating in the inbreaking reign of God. As a fulfilment of the promise of jubilee, "Jesus, through his proclamation and ministry, inaugurates this new jubilee community, and it is this very dynamic the Ephesians writer now describes as Christ's gathering all things into himself. To be saved means that the gathering work of Christ has now also reached you: that you are knitted into the fabric of the new humanity, that you are incorporated into the new household of God" (van Driel).

Van Driel believes that Guder's strong emphasis on mission being at the heart of the church's identity and purpose is exactly right but that the concrete reality of the Christian community, joined to Christ by the Spirit, is the end rather than the means. It is hard to get away from *gathering/sending* language, but it may be that we distinguish that which is essentially one. To keep this dichotomy at the center of our ecclesiology and liturgy "invites the thought that 'mission' is still different from the community's own common life," says van Driel. "But according to the Ephesians letter, the church is sent, the church is witness, the church is on a mission, exactly in its being gathered, in its being knitted together, in its living together as a new household. In this being gathered, in this common life, the church makes visible to the world what the good news of Jesus Christ is all about. To be gathered is to be sent" (van Driel).

In thinking through how this idea of sending and gathering could shape the life of new worshiping communities, there are a couple of crucial implications. The first is the emphasis on *all* being gathered. One of the potential weaknesses of new worshiping communities is the flipside of their strength: they are highly contextual, mostly small communities. How can such communities not be shaped by the larger context where people are normally divided by race, nationality, class, or other basic divisions? It is possible for intentionally contextual communities to embody, rather than challenge, such divisions.[9] The sign that such divisions are overcome in Christian communities is a sign that the reign of God is indeed breaking in.

A multifaceted research project is tracking all aspects of the new worshiping communities initiative. It has yielded some helpful insight into the cultural context into which new worshiping communities are born:

> In addition to having more overall diversity, NWCs are also more likely to have a diverse membership within any given community. If we categorize any worshiping community in which no single race comprises more than 79% of its membership as "racially diverse" (an admittedly low standard to begin with), then only 5% of PC(USA) congregations are racially diverse. In contrast, 68% of NWCs are racially diverse.
>
> Additionally, although NWCs are more likely than congregations to be racially diverse, they are also more likely to be predominantly of a single non-White race or ethnicity. In other words, there is a greater percentage of NWCs that are not racially diverse, but they also are not mostly White. For example, 11% of NWCs have 80% or more participants that are Hispanic or Latinx.[10]

A related implication is the identity of new worshiping communities within denominational identities. We must keep the focus on calling forth new disciples into new communities to be in service to God's greater mission of gathering all in and reconciling all things to God in Christ. This means that extending denominational beachheads is not a goal. New worshiping communities must find ways to offer the best gifts that their denominational traditions have to offer without extending the competitive culture that marks the establishment of new congregations. Focusing on new mission while fostering cooperative ventures between communities of various denominations would mirror the reign of God we proclaim.

Despite such significant challenges, research indicates that 42 percent of the participants in new worshiping communities were not previously engaged in any kind of worshiping community.[11] Making new disciples is more than just a phrase to our new worshiping communities. They are discovering a ripe harvest field. In addition, partnerships with other denominations are common in the new communities.

The central promise to this further integration of gathering and sending is the way that the common life of Christians in Christian communities becomes central to the community's missional identity. The formation of disciples in a community is more than preparation for mission; that formation into a community is integral to the community's witness. "The Christian community does then not just engage in public worship; it engages in public life. In that context it should be clear that being gathered involves much more than being gathered for the Sunday morning service. But this then raises the very question of how new (and old!) worshiping communities can be shaped so that their common life adheres to the Ephesians' vision" (van Driel).

COMMUNITIES OF GRATITUDE

While the term *missional* is sometimes misused so much as to be unhelpful, the core impulse behind it is essential for the new worshiping communities movement: that our communal life as believers is lived for the sake of the whole creation. God's mission precedes any mission we might have. The triune God calls all to the glory of living in relationship with God. The gracious God that we know in Jesus Christ desires to bring all things into the circle of divine love. This means that all Christian communities are marked by gratitude for the gracious love found in Jesus Christ, and witness to that love in the power of the Spirit is at the very heart of the life of the Christian community.

Sentness is at the core of the church's identity and purpose. But what is humanity itself created for? We are created by God for community, with God and one another. The very point of this missional impulse is to restore us to communal relation to God and to one another, a relationship that is restored through the worship of God. The discussion has focused on the Latin term *missio Dei* (the mission of God). In new worshiping communities, we see at the very core of our lives a phenomenon known by another Latin term: *communion Dei* (the communion of God). The mission grows out of the communal character of God, and the character of God always points to the gathering up of all into the divine relationship. To be "saved" is to be brought close, to be brought into the life of God through the people of God. This is the *telos* of grace.

The language of gratitude may be of real help to us here. What we desire in these new communities are people formed together in response to the gracious love of God, people whose communal life and mission are a witness to God. If the Christian life consists of gratitude for the gracious love of God, our communities therefore must be marked by gratitude—gratitude that evokes worship of the one true God, gratitude for the Spirit's work to knit us together as one, and gratitude that recognizes that the community does not exist for its own sake but for the sake of the world.

6

Worshiping: Word and Sacrament

Because the 1001 New Worshiping Communities initiative is an effort to find new ways to carry out Christ's mission, there is no consensus as to the role of Word and sacrament in the worship experience. The place of Word and sacrament is a live question in the engagement around new forms of Christian community.

What does a new community look like? No longer is it a young pastor in a black robe preaching in a new sanctuary in a suburban community. What if there is no preaching at the beginning of the community? What if the community is not practicing baptism or celebrating the Lord's Supper? Are community and mission enough?

These questions provide us an opportunity to revisit the notions of Word and sacrament. Why have they been so central to the church for centuries? These questions also give us the opportunity to consider how new communities form today. The new, exciting work in new worshiping communities will be strengthened by a deepened commitment to Word and sacrament.

WHY WORD AND SACRAMENT WERE SUCH A BIG DEAL DURING THE REFORMATION

John Calvin stands at the heart of the emphasis on Word and sacrament. In one of his most well-known passages, he says, "From this the face of the church comes forth and becomes visible to our eyes. Wherever we see the Word of God purely preached and heard, and the sacraments administered according to Christ's institution, there, it is not to be doubted, a church of God exists."[1] Why would he make this claim? What is at stake for Calvin?

The Church Is Our Mother

One of Calvin's treasured metaphors for the church was *mother*. Calvin agreed with St. Augustine that the church is the mother of believers. Why mother? Mother implies that the Holy Spirit works through the church to birth believers, and the church guides and nurtures believers throughout their lives.[2]

Mother is a strong metaphor, one that can be startling in our context. How many Facebook posts begin, "Why [millennials/young people/ urban dwellers/people committed to justice/those who grew up in the church] are fed up with the church"? In a real sense, that is exactly the situation Calvin saw. He was deeply disappointed with the state of the church, yet he believed that God promises to work through it.

What do we do with such a claim? Because *church* is so identified with institutions, this high view of the church strikes many folks as wide of the mark. Let's get some things off the table: No one is arguing for the necessity of the Presbyterian Church (U.S.A.) or any denomination, even the Roman Catholic Church or Orthodox Churches. Because many of us are suspicious of institutions, the discussion of the centrality of the church quickly descends into anti-institutional concerns. So let's back up a moment.

The nub of Calvin's concern is that God is about forming a people. Throughout Scripture, we see that this is so. It is clear in the formation of the people of Israel. It is the heart of the message of liberation in the exodus story: "I'll take you as my people, and I'll be your God" (Exod. 6:7 CEB). It is also at the heart of the message of Jesus. He calls twelve disciples, a symbol of the people of Israel, and forms them into a community of disciples. Paul echoes the language of Exodus as he addresses the believers in Corinth: "We are the temple of the living God. Just as God said, 'I live with them, and I will move among them. I will be their God, and they will be my people'" (2 Cor. 6:16 CEB). God forms us in a community. It is in community that believers are born, and it is in community that we live out our lives as disciples. Even the hermits of the early church were sustained by communities. We need the Christian community. We need a real community, not an idea of a community.

Because we have such institutional connotations to *church*, it is helpful to substitute *people of God* or *Christian community* when discussing the necessity of the church. It changes the nature of the discussion and reminds us that Christian faith is not solitary faith.

The Need to Locate the People of God

The story of God's interaction with humanity is the story of the formation of a people. Sometimes the Christian faith is described as the story of individuals finding salvation from God; however, the narratives of Scripture show us that God is about a people. If community is at the heart of God's movement toward us, then we need signs or marks to identify the community of the people of God. If the church is our mother in *this* life, it must be concrete; it must be visible. Sometimes Christians talk about the "real church" as some spiritual entity that we can't feel or touch. The story of Scripture calls us to a concrete gathering of Christians in community.

There are churches all over the place. Which church is the true church? Within the Reformation context this question was important.

We Don't Know Who Belongs

Another important factor for Calvin was the limits of human judgment. My sense is that today many of us believe we can discern what is in another person's heart, being able to judge their motives. Calvin did not. He thought that human beings were incapable of determining the deepest thoughts and feelings of another. We cannot know another person's true will. Because we cannot make ultimate judgments, we must regard one another with generosity. Since only God can know these things, we are modest about the extent of our judgments within the Christian community. In short, we give one another the benefit of the doubt. In short, we cannot identify the church by looking at particular persons and saying, "Those people are the true church."

How Not to Find the People of God

One of the difficulties of reading Reformation-era texts in our day is the consistent trashing of Roman Catholics by Protestants and of Protestants by Roman Catholics. These mutual condemnations don't make a lot of sense to us today, but we need to explore how Calvin criticized the Roman Catholic Church to understand how he conceived of the church.

Calvin believed that the corruption of the Roman Catholic Church in his time demonstrated that one cannot find this true, visible church on the basis of institutional form, age, episcopal succession, or doctrinal consensus.[3] To put it in a more contemporary context, the fact that a church is called Presbyterian, Episcopal, Methodist, Christian, the Master's Table, First, Westminster, Aldersgate, or St. Pius does not mean it is a true church—nor does the fact that it claims to be "Bible believing" and meets at the neighborhood bar.

How to Find the People of God

We need signs of the Christian community, things we can experience with our five senses that point us in the right direction. Calvin identified two marks most clearly: Word and sacrament. The marks of Word and sacrament are empirical evidence, available to any who seek, to describe practices that ensure Christ is present in that church's ministry: "[God has] set off by plainer marks the knowledge of his very body to us, knowing how necessary it is to our salvation."[4]

Why Word and Sacrament?

It is easy to make a list of things desired in a Christian community. Why would Calvin settle on these two? Calvin believed that Word and sacrament were means of grace that ensure we will find Christ at work: "For it is certain that such things [Word and sacrament] are not without fruit."[5] This is a crucial point. While there are many aspects of a church we might desire, how do we know God is at work in this community? "From this the face of the church comes forth and becomes visible to our eyes. Wherever we see the Word of God

purely preached and heard, and the sacraments administered according to Christ's institution, there, it is not to be doubted, a church of
God exists."[6]

These marks are not a definition of the church. They are not even
a minimal definition of a Christian community. These marks—
a gathered community, a practice of ministry, and the authority of
Scripture—assume that a form of Christian community already exists.
Word and sacrament are not enough for a Christian community. They
are a means to discern a faithful community.

WHAT ABOUT PREACHING?

The language for 1001 New Worshiping Communities speaks only of
"gathering around Word and sacrament" without the classic language
that the Word should be "purely preached." This is a good change. The
idea is not to undercut the faithful exposition of the Word within the
congregation but rather to unleash the Word (for the Spirit to speak),
and that can happen in a variety of forms.

At Isaiah's Table in Syracuse, New York, the word is usually proclaimed through dialogue around the breakfast table. Conversation
partners include Presbyterian ruling elders, homeless men, and neighborhood children. At the Open Door in Pittsburgh, community members often respond to the reading of the Word through participating
in group art projects that are shared with the wider community. The
Word needs to be proclaimed, but preaching is not the only way to
proclaim the Word.

CHALLENGES TO REFORMATION MARKS

In previous models of forming new congregations, it was easy to identify the centrality of Word and sacrament since the first act of the new
congregation was almost always corporate worship. When the land
was acquired, the minister secured, and the building built, the first
act was a worship service, which often included celebrating at the
Lord's Table. The plan was for the church to develop a full-orbed
mission and ministry, but worship, centered in Word and sacrament,
was the hub.

One thing that distinguishes new worshiping communities is that they can begin with any act within the life of the community: mission, fellowship, shared affinity, worship, service, Bible study, and so forth. In effect, new worshiping communities rely on another promise: "For where two or three are gathered in my name, I am there among them" (Matt 18:20). It is in the presence of two or three that the community is gathered. And while the hope is that new worshiping communities will become full congregations, we know that some will not.

What we are seeing in new worshiping communities is not so much a relativization of Word and sacrament but a nonlinear understanding of how we get there. Word and sacrament may be first, in the middle, or at the end of a community's journey. Many new worshiping communities gather for months, building relationships and sharing life together before finding a rhythm of worship that works. There may be a pattern of formal, pastoral leadership at the beginning or at the end, or there may be a model where pastoral leadership is shared with other communities and/or congregations, more like an early church bishop than our accustomed model of the installed pastor.

DISCIPLINE

In the 1550s, Calvin dispensed a fair amount of ecclesiastical advice to the nascent Protestant church in France. Calvin was supportive of their efforts but believed that the loose structure of French Protestantism would not provide long-term viability. He doubted that the climate in France would allow for the immediate formation of a church modeled on the church of Geneva. He was concerned that a church that could not practice discipline could not appropriately preach the Word and administer the sacraments. What should the French Protestants do? Calvin consistently advised them to continue in small group meetings and not to draw up doctrinal or ecclesiastical accords. But such advice made no provision for sacraments. And Calvin resolutely opposed celebrating either baptism or the Lord's Supper in such a context. If sharing in the sacraments was necessary, he advised traveling to Geneva, where the pure Word of God was preached and the true sacraments celebrated.[7]

Calvin was convinced that these French Protestants were faithful. He commended them for their continued fidelity to God in a place where such commitments exposed them to what he referred to as "the dangers which may perhaps be about to occur to you, owing to the malice of your adversaries."[8] However, their fidelity to the gospel was not sufficient to allow them to celebrate the sacraments. Instead, Calvin instructed them that they should not be "in a hurry" to celebrate the sacraments until there was an order established among them. The "form of a church" was required.

The faithful in France were incapable of receiving the sacraments within their own fellowships until they were properly ordered. In fact, in this period Calvin advised Protestants in France to have their children baptized by Catholic priests rather than have them baptized in an improper manner by someone other than a minister who has been elected and chosen by the people in an ordered church.[9]

Sharing of material possessions and common study of the Bible was encouraged for the bands of believers,[10] but celebration of the sacraments was to be delayed until a solid foundation had been built.

We're a long way from the emphasis on discipline in sixteenth-century Geneva. Intervening practices such as Communion tokens soured our tradition on strict discipline, to the point that the new PC(USA) Directory for Worship includes language that acknowledges the fact that the nonbaptized come to the table: "The opportunity to eat and drink with Christ is not a right bestowed upon the worthy, but a privilege given to the undeserving who come in faith, repentance, and love. All who come to the table are offered the bread and cup, regardless of their age or understanding. If some of those who come have not yet been baptized, an invitation to baptismal preparation and baptism should be graciously extended."[11]

Without getting too caught up in the details, Calvin's insistence on discipline is vital, especially when we tie it to the related word *discipleship*. That is, proclaiming the Word and celebrating the sacraments may be ways to identify the church, but for them to flower we need the response of the people in committed discipleship. This is the force of the short phrase "and heard" in Calvin's description.

One of our opportunities with new worshiping communities is to reengage with the practice of hearing and living out the gospel. It is an opportunity to commit to communal accountability and encouragement within the body of Christ. Few practices would be more transformative for new worshiping communities and congregations in general.[12]

ADMINISTERED ACCORDING TO CHRIST'S INSTITUTION: THE ROLE OF PASTORS

We also see in this vignette the importance of the pastor. One of the biggest hurdles for new worshiping communities around Word and sacrament is leadership, particularly around sacraments. Like many denominations, the Presbyterian Church (U.S.A.) has rules concerning who can celebrate sacraments within a congregation. That is, only a minister of the Word and Sacrament or a commissioned ruling elder (CRE) can celebrate at the Lord's Table or baptize. Other denominations may use different terminology, but most have similar practices. In the case of the PC(USA), a CRE needs to have been elected as a ruling elder in a constituted congregation before serving as a CRE for another community. We have traditionally lifted up the role of teaching elder all the while affirming the possibility that any believer can proclaim the Word of God to a gathered community—but not so much with the sacraments. The language in the new Directory for Worship reads, "The Lord's Supper shall be authorized by the session and administered by a minister of Word and Sacrament," but with the caveat that "the functions described as belonging to teaching elders may be, in particular circumstances, also performed by ruling elders."[13]

One of the questions before us in this project is how we continue to hold to this classic understanding of Word and sacrament in new worshiping communities. How do we propose that Word and sacrament be practiced in communities that do not have a theologically educated pastor who has been installed in the community?

But we are far from sixteenth-century France in time, distance, and culture. New worshiping communities are not growing on an isolated frontier but rather in the midst of a vast network of churches seeking to be faithful. The 1001 initiative emphasizes the connectional nature of the church in a relationship of "care and accountability." When new worshiping communities are unable to offer sacramental celebration due to the lack of ordained leadership, the wider church steps in to offer help. The nurturing relationship with a partner congregation or a midcouncil provides the oversight needed for the administration of baptisms and the Lord's Supper. This is a relationship of mutuality in which the organized congregation absorbs some of the new life and energy of the new worshiping community while the new worshiping community leans on the rich history and tradition of its partner congregation.

CLOSING THOUGHTS

It is good that Word, sacrament, and discipline have made it into the 1001 initiative definition, even if in stealth form, because they underline our conviction of pointing to Christ as the center of our communities and thereby relativizing our institutions appropriately. Likewise, the language of *gathered* is appropriate because, more so than the sixteenth-century discussion, it situates these marks in the gathered community. In a time when the church's identity increasingly needs to be understood and practiced in contrast to the wider community, this is helpful language. May the Christ who calls this church into being shape these communities through the Holy Spirit.

7

Worshiping: Sent by the Spirit

One of the cornerstone convictions of the new worshiping communities movement is that believers in Jesus Christ are sent by the Spirit. The gift that missional theology has given the church is to insist that *sentness* is fundamental to the church's identity. We are sent. We, as a community, are sent.

Oh, would that it were true. Despite the missional force behind the dismissal, there's no doubt that in many gatherings for worship, the dismissal signals, "That's all until next time." If the gathering is integral to the sending, if we are gathered, at least in great part, to be equipped to be sent, how are we sent? In this chapter, we will focus on what it means to be sent as a community.

It is important that we consider the concept of sending as a community in contrast to the scattering of individuals. In much of our culture, we are so oriented toward being individuals that it is hard to imagine how a community bears the missional call. We can think about actions such as mission projects—that is easy enough to do. But it is much harder for us to conceive of how the community, as a community, is *sent* in our ordinary lives between Sundays.

Why focus on practice in local communities? Stanley Hauerwas writes that Christians grow as disciples of Christ, that they learn to live justly "by imitating just persons." He continues: "One way of teaching good habits is by watching good people, learning the moves, imitating the way they relate to the world." This cuts against the way we often do formation in the church, where we teach, in principle, how Christians behave. Sometimes we just want to teach in a rational manner what it looks like to practice being a Christian, but Hauerwas reminds us that "nothing in the Sermon on the Mount suggests that the way of disciples is 'rational.'"[1] At the same time, community by itself doesn't teach us to follow Jesus. We need the teachings of Scripture and the long history of the church. Communities themselves can be toxic or inert. Hauerwas's point isn't that we need community, full stop. It is that we need communities formed by Jesus:

> But just as the Christian faith has no stake in people being a part of just any old community, so we have no stake in people affirming any old tradition. Traditions can be less and more true. They can also be false and lead to the false security, the arrogant claims of those who presume to be different from others on the basis of shallow pronouncements about an often false memory.[2]

The hard conclusion of this understanding of practicing Christian faith is that it takes work, it takes training, it takes imitation, and it takes the formation of habits, because living like Christ "is not something that comes naturally." Observing the lives of the saints provides concrete examples to consider and presents "us with a wider array of ethical possibilities than we would have had if left to our own devices."[3]

THE COMMUNITY AS SENT

When we consider the notion of the community being sent, the biggest obstacle for many of us is that we are really not a community to begin with. There is no choice to be made about strengthening the gathered community over against being sent forth in mission. As discussed in chapter 5, there is an integral relationship between the character of the community and its mission. The character of the gathered community is mission.

Of course, there are many counterexamples of this: those communities that focus only on their long-term survival and have no sense of being sent by the Spirit into the world. We all know stories of the dying church where members hope the doors stay open through their funerals but have no larger vision. Such stories are not only the stories of communities that have lost their vision for God's mission but also stories of communities that have lost their sense of being communities, where the very character of the gathered saints is a witness to the *missio Dei.*

We will look at the lives of the saints in two places in this chapter, drawing on the wisdom and experience of Libby Tedder Hugus, a worshiping community leader from Casper, Wyoming.

THE TABLE IN CASPER, WYOMING

Embracing the apostolic vocation requires that we begin to see our story as interwoven in God's story. It requires that we begin to see the risk and reward of following Jesus as central to our identity as disciples. Hugus speaks poignantly of how this began for her at a young age.

> Puppet shows mesmerized me as a kid. Something about the peach-fuzz characters with their googly eyes and cartoon voices captured my imagination. From time to time in the church of my childhood in Omaha, Nebraska, puppets were used to communicate God's story. I have this vivid memory from one particular show when, with gaping mouths and imaginary spit flying, the puppets sang Scott Wesley Brown and Phill McHugh's "Please Don't Send Me to Africa." The sarcastically ridiculous lyrics are a plea with God to be allowed to serve from cozy, middle-class America rather than in Africa. The singer goes on to bargain an 11 percent tithe in exchange for not being sent into the jungle where the locals are restless at night.
>
> That song lodged in my memory because of the lenses through which I view the world. By cultural descent I am half–South African and half-American (USA), and I maintain dual citizenship. My brother and I both were born in Johannesburg, South Africa. We moved to Omaha when I was three years old and back to South Africa when I was fourteen years old. My dad is fourth-generation South African, and all the members of the paternal side of my family remain in South Africa. My mom was raised from birth until age seventeen in sub-Saharan Africa as the daughter of American missionaries. Before entering university, I had lived in four nations: South Africa, the United States, Malawi, and Kenya. The puppet's silly song was meant to be the satirical (and prejudiced) reaction of a suburban American to God's missional call. If I were to sing the song, I would be asking God not to send me home. Somewhere in my child psyche, I intuited

how this was the opposite of God's aim in the world. Asking God not
to send you somewhere is anti-gospel. (Hugus)

Asking God not to send you somewhere is anti-gospel. This may well
be the tagline of the 1001 New Worshiping Communities initiative.
It succinctly captures the insights of the missional movement—that
being caught up in God's activity in the world is not the province of the
specially called but is the province of all the baptized.

We find our stories in God's story. "God is the seminal missionary:
God sends, creation is sent. Jesus commissions, disciples are sent. The
Spirit breathes, followers are sent" (Hugus). Hugus finds the primary
themes of this story in the Genesis creation account and in John's Gospel. She reads this creation story in a Trinitarian fashion, noting how
God's spirit was "hovering over the face of the water" (Gen. 1:2 NLT).
"God's spirit breathed in and out over the primordial soup and from
the chaos sprung life. The Trinitarian God—the parent, the child, and
the spirit—breathed and creation came to be, and all that God breathes
into being is good" (Hugus). This creation moment is the first indica-
tion of God's character, the God who is for us,[4] the one who breathed
into us the breath of life.

In John's Gospel, when Jesus gifts the Holy Spirit to the terrified
disciples on the night of his resurrection, he gives them words of assurance and peace, and he combines that peace with their vocation, their
sentness: "Peace be with you. As the Father has sent me, so I am sending you." They are sent out, not in their own power, but by the very
power that raised Jesus from the dead. Then Jesus breathes on them
and says, "Receive the Holy Spirit. If you forgive anyone's sins, they
are forgiven. If you do not forgive them, they are not forgiven" (John
20:22–23 NLT). Lest we overromanticize this gift of the Spirit, Hugus
grounds the act in everyday earthiness.

> Have you ever wondered what Jesus' breath smelled like when he
> breathed on his disciples? It may strike you as offensive or even
> creepy at first. Breath is intimate and could very well be stinky! God's
> breath is intimate; it gives life. Being near enough to Jesus to know
> his scent is intimate. Jesus' breath, like the Spirit's, must have been
> reminiscent of the very moment in creation when life blossomed
> from the unknown—like a jolt of minty freshness and newly blos-
> somed flowers and the earth just after the rain all rolled into one
> empowering puff. (Hugus)

We can count on the apostle Paul to provide a more theological description of being sent: "It is God who enables us, along with you, to stand firm for Christ. He has commissioned us, and he has identified us as his own by placing the Holy Spirit in our hearts as the first installment that guarantees everything he has promised us" (2 Cor. 1:21–22 NLT).

Since at least the middle of the 20th century, the term *missio Dei,* or *mission of God,* has been a central theological description of the character of God's work. Correspondingly, the church's efforts have been described less in terms of *doing* God's mission than in *joining* God's mission. South African theologian David Bosch claims that God's church doesn't have a mission; God's mission has a church.[5] Hugus ties this understanding to new worshiping communities and to the work of the church in general: "The church is a servant of God's grand, comprehensive mission. That mission is gospel, and it is already well under way. The gospel (the really, really good news) runs the depth and breadth of creation aiming for the reconciliation of all things" (Hugus).

The amazing thing about this call is that it comes immediately from God to us. It is not something we receive only when we are mature or experienced.

> When God called Abram, they were not yet acquainted, when out of nowhere God spoke directly to Abram, "Leave your native country, your relatives, and your father's family, and go to the land that I will show you. I will make you into a great nation. I will bless you and make you famous, and you will be a blessing to others. I will bless those who bless you and curse those who treat you with contempt. All the families on earth will be blessed through you." (Gen. 12:1–3 NLT)

Hugus refers to an African proverb: "When you pray, move your feet." This proverb concisely connects worship, prayer, and gathering to sending, mission, and apostolic vocation. Abram was called and acted. When God said go, he joined the mission, moving his feet in response to divine instruction. Hugus puts this call to mission in poetic form:

> We pray because Jesus taught us how to relocate our awareness of who God is and who we are. We pray because we need to experience the compassion of our heavenly parent. We pray because it sharpens our intentions and makes us better listeners. We pray because it heals us of blind unbelief and opens our eyes to God's will on earth.

We pray because we remember our true dependence when naming our daily needs: bread, forgiveness, peace with neighbors, and protection from trial.

We pray because we need help to see where the leavening yeast of God's grace is being kneaded into every nook and cranny of creation. We pray so that when God's redemption is baked into our very lives and begins to rise throughout the world, we can share it with the hungry.[6]

The goal of this mission is immense: the transformation of the world. This is a huge end game when we think about it in relation to new worshiping communities, most of which are small. Hugus reminds us that Abram's call was also a huge mission given to a relatively insignificant people: "When sending Abram, God began a global transformation aiming to bless each family with reconciliation. This was not exclusively for Abram and his descendants; this was for all the families on earth" (Hugus). Hugus uses an extended metaphor of the baking of bread to illustrate.

> Have you ever noticed how bread isn't bread until it is baked? The flour, water, yeast, and salt remain inert until the baker sets to work. The baker combines the ingredients, kneads the dough, allows it to ferment and proof, forms the dough into the suggested hint of its final form, and finally places it in the oven. While it is baking, it is becoming bread. It is a hidden, miraculous transformation into bread. When we worship through prayer, when we really listen to baker God and relocate our awareness of love, when God's redemption is baked into our own lives individually and communally, we are transformed into the Bread of Life. This hidden, miraculous transformation of regular, old humans into Christ's body means that bits and pieces of the Bread of Life can be broken off and fed to the hungry. We become the trail of crumbs leading the way back to the one who satisfies our hunger and is transforming our world from food desert into banquet feast.
>
> In worship, like breathing, we are inhaled into God's loving presence and exhaled to carry breath to our love-deprived world. If worshiping communities refuse to oxygenate the world with God's love, the literal lifeblood of the church will be poisoned. If lovers of God hoard the Bread of Life selfishly, the nourishing manna will spoil.
>
> God sends us to participate in a mission far greater than the sum of the parts of any community, congregation, movement, or denomination. God's blessing was not exclusive to Abram's family.

Neither was the good news of God's salvation only for those frightened disciples huddled together on the night of Jesus' resurrection or for those earliest adopting apostles. Christopher Wright describes the whole world as the goal, scope, and arena of God's mission in which we are invited to participate.[7] The Lausanne Covenant claims "world evangelization requires the whole church to take the whole gospel to the whole world."[8] A mission of this scope has geographical, ecological, economic, social, and political ramifications. God's mission is for the sake of the transformation of the entire world: all peoples, all cultures, all places, all creatures. (Hugus)

The story of the Table in Casper, Wyoming, illustrates the sending Spirit.

The Table is a new worshiping community God breathed to life in 2014 in Casper, Wyoming. It was birthed out of a weekly common meal hosted during cold Wyoming winters in my home, together with my husband and housemates, called Souper Tuesdays. My husband and I began to notice in conversations with friends over steaming bowls of soup and fresh crusty bread that there was an entire swath of people in Casper who had deep questions about what matters in life and about God but had no safe place to explore those questions if they were estranged from or unfamiliar with church. So an exploratory team gathered to dream about curating a space for asking those questions. We were lovingly sent to be that kind of community by many faithful congregations, individuals, and the council of the Presbytery of Wyoming. Now we gather weekly as doubters and disciples together making space to pursue nourishment that feeds our whole beings, but not just to gorge ourselves. The Table is sent by God's Spirit as an agent of mission to be the answers to our questions. We have begun to explore community partnerships, including public witness to peace and justice alongside Campaign Nonviolence and hosting local artists during Casper's monthly Art Walk in our downtown neighborhood. Every week a benediction sends us from worship: "Go now to love and serve the world so that those to whom love is a stranger might find in us generous friends." (Hugus)

As communities find their story in God's story, they often root their story in a particular passage of Scripture. The Table's story is rooted in Jeremiah 29. At this point in the history of Israel, Israel is a nation in exile. The Babylonian conquest has brought shame and humiliation. The Israelite captives have no place set aside for worship and cannot live under the law of Moses, their communal bonds that enabled obedience having been broken. They most likely are looking for words of judgment against their oppressors when Jeremiah speaks the word of the Lord, but they hear something quite different:

> Jeremiah wrote a letter from Jerusalem to the elders, priests, prophets, and all the people who had been exiled to Babylon by King Nebuchadnezzar. . . . This is what Jeremiah's letter said:
>
> This is what the Lord of Heaven's Armies, the God of Israel, says to all the captives he has exiled to Babylon from Jerusalem: "Build homes, and plan to stay. Plant gardens, and eat the food they produce. Marry and have children. Then find spouses for them so that you may have many grandchildren. Multiply! Do not dwindle away! And work for the peace and prosperity of the city where I sent you into exile. Pray to the Lord for it, for its welfare will determine your welfare." (Jer. 29:1–7 NLT)

Instead of hearing a word of retribution or triumph over enemies, the exiles were asked to see their future in Babylon. "God was calling them to become a force for good, a blessing to their captors. They were called to put down roots rather than wither away. God, in this message to Israel, was calling them back to the promise made to their forefather, Abram, 'You will be a blessing to others. . . . All the families on earth will be blessed through you'" (Hugus). Hugus believes that this call to the exiles is a call to contemporary worshiping communities.

> Praying for and working for the peace of our cities and countrysides means learning to love our enemies, learning to work for the common good of the whole. Wherever God calls us is home because there too is God's Spirit; there too is God's redemption. No one is exempt from the blessing of God's transforming mission. According to Jeremiah's warning, the welfare of the cities (and countrysides) in which we reside depends on the extent to which we work for the peace of the whole community, indeed the whole world.

The people of Judah were being sent, even though that sentness was to change their orientation right where they were.

> Prior to hearing Jeremiah's warning, the Hebrews would have probably resonated with the goofy puppet's song of my childhood, preferring lyrics like, 'Please don't send me to Babylon where the barbarians are restless at night.' But what kind of song could they sing after hearing God's words through Jeremiah's letter? (Hugus)

New worshiping communities can help lead the larger church to deeper embodiment of the apostolic vocation. They are worshiping communities, which means that they are sent by the Spirit to join God's mission for the transformation of the world. This sending has been going on since the creation. "Breathed into the shared life of God, new worshiping communities are breathed out to oxygenate the world with saving love, God's generous gift of reconciliation," says Hugus. "New worshiping communities are sent into mission to join forces with God's transformation already at work across the globe, even the universe." God's Spirit is working through all peoples and cultures across the globe. We align ourselves with God's reality, the reality that all things will be drawn together. We join in God's mission, sent by the Spirit, for the transformation of the world. "The 1001 New Worshiping Communities movement does not sing the sarcastic puppet song of yesteryear. We sing the song of Isaiah, who, when God asks, 'Whom should I send as a messenger to the people? Who will go for us?' respond, 'Here we are, send us!'" (Hugus).

8

COMMUNITIES of Care and Accountability

The saints help us to live as Christians together. By *saints* we mean those Christians whose lives are marked by a kind of faithfulness that we can emulate, whether they are recognized by a church formally or not. In this chapter, we'll focus on the lives of the saints, past and present, to expand our possibilities of what it means to live as a community of Christians. We'll meet some saints in sixteenth-century Geneva and in twenty-first-century Pittsburgh.

The term *community* is vital to the new worshiping community effort. It is not a placeholder or a way to avoid saying *church* or *congregation*. Instead, *community* profoundly describes the character of our relationship to God and to one another. It is a way to underline the character that congregations should have but don't always. In other words, *community* is the more primary word for what we often call *congregations*. Dutch author Stefan Paas suggests that the word *church* may be too confining for an infant community:

> Wouldn't it be better to have a more flexible vocabulary that appreciates such activities (as worship, mission or community-building) as possibly legitimate and valuable expressions of mission or worship, without the need to call them "church"—at least not right away? Certainly, such a vocabulary would have the potential of inviting more people on board when it comes to new Christian community formation.[1]

This chapter consists of three parts: a reflection on practices of community in the sixteenth-century Reformed movement, a discussion of contemporary challenges to community, and a conversation with Christopher Brown on the practices of community in the new worshiping community he helped to lead.

THE BEST WE HAVE TO OFFER

When I (Vera) was still new to the world of church planting, I gathered together a group of pioneer leaders and presbytery stalwarts for a day to discuss how new churches and the traditional church could work together for the benefit of all. At the end of a rich day of learning and collaboration, I asked the following question to the new worshiping community leaders: "What do you really need from the established church?" My assumption was that the response would be "money." After all, I had never seen a brand-new church that didn't struggle with finances. Instead, I was surprised to hear one leader respond, "We need you to keep us accountable."

With the need for accountability in mind, let us look at lessons learned from the Reformation period in Geneva as a window into the history and theology of discipline in the Reformed tradition. The word *discipline* may raise a red flag for you because we tend to use words like *inclusive* or *accepting* to describe an attractive community, but these are not opposite ends of a spectrum.

When people think of John Calvin and church discipline, they often picture a man named Michael Servetus being burned at the stake to enforce doctrinal and moral purity. One of the reasons that one episode is so prominent is because it was the only instance of burning at the stake during Calvin's time in Geneva. Of course, we wouldn't want to rest too easy in the rarity of a burning at the stake, but it is worth taking note of in an age when stake burnings were all too common. This picture was sharpened by the scholars who translated the Registers of the Consistory, the records of how church discipline was practiced in Geneva. The most sensational episodes were the only ones published, so for centuries people thought that discipline was all about doctrinal or salacious moral offenses. Over the past few decades we've learned that discipline was far more ordinary.

John Calvin's first effort to reform the church in Geneva was less than successful. One of the principal causes for opposition to Calvin's reform was his insistence that the people take Communion every week in worship; under the previous Catholic regime, the people received the elements only once a year. Because of deep-seated resistance to a reformation of all church life, Calvin departed for Strasbourg, France, where Martin Bucer mentored him. Under Bucer, Calvin grasped that a reformation of the church called for the practice of discipline for all people in the church.

A few years later when the situation in Geneva had become desperate, the city fathers called Calvin back to continue the reform of the church. In preparing to return, Calvin pressed for a number of concrete reforms. Again, he requested weekly Communion, but this time he insisted strongly on disciplinary practices around the table. The city leaders balked at the extent of Calvin's demands. Calvin finally relented on weekly Communion (against his better judgment), but he would not compromise on the establishment of a consistory that would ensure a discipline around the table that grows out of the promises made at baptism.

While the faithful proclamation of the Word and the right celebration of the sacraments were at the center of church practice for Calvin, he recognized that discipline was necessary for holding these practices together. In his famous reply to Cardinal Sadeleto, bishop of Carpentras in Southern France, Calvin wrote that discipline held the church together: "For the body of the Church, to cohere well, must be bound together by discipline as with sinews."[2]

Central to the Reformed tradition from its very inception is a commitment to the faithful living of Christian faith coupled with an admission that such faithfulness is not possible alone. In the church we need each other—we must be accountable to each other—to live faithful lives.

The church in our own time is entering a new age, perhaps in the end as dramatic a shift as the Reformation was in its time. After four and a half centuries of ascending importance within Western culture, Christian churches are learning that they are no longer in control of the culture but need to learn to live as a minority within the larger culture. As we enter this new time, our identity is at stake, not for its own sake, but for the sake of being faithful to our Savior, Jesus Christ. In such a context, a biblical practice of discipline is required.

ORDINARY DISCIPLINE

The great achievement of our Reformed forebears was the recovery of ordinary discipline. Ordinary, not extraordinary, discipline was the preoccupation of Reformers such as Calvin. Ordinary discipline is the practice of the church to assist Christians to stay true to their deepest desires, desires given to them by God—to live a faithful Christian life, to stay true to the vows made at baptism.

Ordinary discipline was Calvin's preoccupation, although he clearly believed in and practiced extraordinary discipline. Preceding the time of the Reformation, discipline was primarily exercised in two ways. The first was extraordinary discipline of heresy trials and the like against people who were accused of opposing the church's teaching or standards. Extraordinary discipline involves either holding someone to their vows against their wishes or resolving a dispute between parties where there is no agreement on the good. The second was special discipline for those in religious vocations (monks, nuns, and others in religious orders) that went well beyond what was expected of the average Christian. In fact, the extraordinary discipline of the late medieval period has significant continuity with that exercised by the Reformers.

Calvin took the special discipline restricted to those in religious vocations and extended it to every believer. He rejected the notion that only those who had taken vows of celibacy were to live truly disciplined lives. In a real sense, Calvin extended the monastery to the whole church, expecting every Christian to submit his or her own life to Christ in all aspects of life. Echoes of this emphasis exist in discussions today about the new monasticism.

Let's look at an example from Geneva in 1542, the account of "Master Michiel the Saddler and His Nephew." (The text is from the minutes of the consistory, the body of ministers and elders that exercised most cases of discipline in the church; it is not composed of polished, complete sentences.)

> Why he and his nephew have been in conflict for a long time, and various other questions. Answers that he pardons his said nephew although he has caused him much pain, and that he will never be in his company, and that he has not taken Communion three or four times because of this quarrel, and that he took it last time. The Consistory, the preachers having given the said Michiel strict admonitions, exhorted him to pardon his said nephew entirely according to the commandment of God for the offenses his said nephew has committed against him for the honor of Jesus Christ. Answers that for the love of God he pardons him entirely for the injuries he has done him. And also that he go to the sermons, and answers that he can hardly go there because he is ill.

The nephew was asked what grudge or resentment he has felt against his uncle for a long time, and other things. Answers that he carries no hate against his uncle and that he does him all the favors he can, but that he is not pleased with him and does not care about him, and that he does him all the honor he can and has begged mercy on his knees from his uncle and he wants to pardon him also, and promises that he will never give any displeasure either to him or his aunt. And they pardoned each other and embraced and expressed love for each other and left together.[3]

This account of Michiel and his nephew is far more typical of discipline in Geneva than heresy trials or other spectacular tales. It was not the arena of burnings at the stake or banishment from the realm; it was the pastoral process of helping people to reconcile with one another in Christ, even uncles and nephews who cannot speak to one another.

Ordinary discipline is the role of the church community in reminding us of what we truly want. In chapter 1 we discussed Augustine's description of the Christian life: "Love God and do what you want." This is not a statement underwriting an "anything goes" account of the Christian life. No—the foundation for church discipline is, ironically, the freedom we have in Christ. It's not that we need to reign in freedom so that we behave correctly but rather that in Christ we are emancipated from our slavery to sin and are free to obey. Discipline becomes a help to us as we exercise our freedom to live godly lives.

It was this ordinary discipline that was at the center of Geneva's ecclesial practices. For Reformed Christians, there is no extraordinary discipline without the practice of ordinary discipline. Extraordinary discipline is only practiced as an outgrowth of ordinary discipline.

Much has changed since the time of the Reformation, but God still calls redeemed sinners to live faithful lives. And we still cannot answer that call on our own strength. We need the life of a disciplined community surrounding us to give us strength to follow.

Reconciliation

Ordinary discipline is local, relational, and restorative. The goal of exercising this discipline is restoration and reconciliation.

It is ordinary discipline that should be at the heart of our practice. Ordinary discipline is community focused, carried out principally by community leaders who know the people in the community. Martin Bucer said that discipline was best handled between friends. Ordinary discipline is a mutual ministry of all the leaders of a community together. The spiritual leaders of a community exercise responsibilities for the spiritual life of that community: counseling with those to be baptized, accepting people into membership, being responsible for the service of the Lord's Table.

In the story of Michiel and his nephew, did you note the asking of forgiveness, the embrace, and the leaving together? Almost every case of church discipline during this period ended in touch appropriate to the relationship of the parties involved: a hug between spouses, a handshake between business partners, and so forth. Ordinary discipline is not about "getting" each other or holding each other's feet to the fire. In ordinary church discipline we care enough about each other to treat one another with respect, with love, and with the will to risk helping each other grow in Christ.

Grace in the Mundane

In ordinary church discipline, most cases are mundane. When people were brought before the consistory in Geneva, the most common offense was not adultery, or prostitution, or heresy, or the other "good ones." It was hate. Hate was the presenting issue in the story of Master Michiel and his nephew. When discipline is solely focused on extraordinary discipline and high-profile offenses, we lose the ability to realize that it is in our everyday lives with each other that our sin seeps out.

This connection between the reception of grace and holy living is expressed well in the French Confession of 1559: "By faith we receive grace to live holy lives in awe and reverence for God, for we receive what the gospel promises when God gives us the Holy Spirit. So faith does not cool our desire for good and holy living, but rather engenders and excites it in us, leading naturally to good works."[4] Because ordinary discipline is centered on the good works that grow naturally from God's grace working in our lives, it is centered on the mundane aspects of our lives. Considering discipline primarily as the extraordinary cases obscures this important aspect of the Christian life.

We Are All Implicated

In an appropriate exercise of ordinary discipline, we are all implicated. Ordinary discipline implicates those who openly sin and those who seem above reproach. Ordinary discipline implicates people of questionable character and successful pastors. Ordinary discipline implicates deacons in a small church and General Assembly staff. We are all implicated. In worship, all of us confess that we

> have lived for ourselves,
> and apart from [God].
> We have turned from our neighbors,
> and refused to bear the burdens of others.
> We have ignored the pain of the world,
> and passed by the hungry, the poor, and the oppressed.[5]

One of the promises of new worshiping communities is that they will help the whole church reclaim biblical practices of being church. The church is not simply a collection of like-minded individuals. When the church is ordered correctly, "pure doctrine can be maintained, vices can be corrected and suppressed, the poor and afflicted can be helped in their need, assemblies can be gathered in the name of God, and both great and small can be edified."[6]

LEARNING FROM THE SAINTS IN PITTSBURGH

Mutual accountability engages all aspects of our lives. While our imaginations are often drawn to the more spectacular, there are aspects of our lives together that are often off-limits. Money is one of those third rails. It is interesting that when Chris Brown of the Upper Room reflects on how he has been held accountable, his first example is about money. As Brown and his copastor, Michael Gehrling, were meeting with the New Church Development Commission of Pittsburgh Presbytery, the challenge came to them not of their prayer for the community, their heart for those with no faith, or their desire to work for justice. The challenge came in the form of this statement: "You need to develop a financial plan." That's the problem with accountability; the questions and the challenges don't necessarily come from the places you expect. For some of us, the financial part would be the easy part, the deeper spiritual discernment more difficult. For Brown and Gehrling, it was the need to become financially self-sustaining as grant funds phased out that was the point of accountability. And this was good news—the members of the commission shared the vision with Brown and Gehrling. It was a good pairing of gifts and oversight. The conclusion was that the presbytery sent them to a stewardship conference, a gift that resulted in an effective stewardship campaign where members of the community responded in generosity, out of gratitude, a turning point in the life of the community.

If new worshiping communities are to practice mutual care and accountability, both must be practiced in the local community and in the relationship to the larger body of Christ. Mutual care is much more pleasant, to be sure. Brown, however, notes that care and accountability are two sides of the same coin. In writing about these matters, seventh-century monk John Climacus said, "Wounds shown in public do not grow worse, but will be healed."[7] The accountability exercised by the presbytery commission was a function of their care for the community. Brown notes, "Mutual care and accountability cannot be practiced without a commitment to lasting relationship. In our case, the lasting relationship was predicated upon the divine reality which all parties involved had received by grace: common baptism into the Body of Christ." (Brown)

WORSHIP AT THE HEART

The exercise of mutual care and accountability is irrevocably related to the worship life of the church: the proclamation of the Word and the administration of the sacraments of baptism and the Lord's Supper. It is in the practice of baptism that we have the foundation for these practices. Brown illustrates this with the baptism of his own children.

> Both of my daughters were baptized at the Upper Room. On Easter 2013 and Pentecost 2015, my wife and I handed a tiny baby girl to my copastor Mike so that he could perform the sacrament that united them to Christ's death and resurrection. After pouring water on their heads, Mike passed each girl further away from us to an elder in our congregation who prayed over them and affirmed the congregation's responsibility for them. Through their baptism, we and the congregation agreed, these children belong not just to Christ but to the whole body of Christ, the church.

> Because by the grace of our common baptism into Christ "we belong to each other" (Rom. 12:5 CEB), we cannot choose to separate ourselves from others who belong to Christ. Cyprian of Carthage, a third-century bishop whose ecclesiology influenced John Calvin's idea of a "presbytery,"[8] wrote that one "cannot have God as his Father who does not have the Church as his Mother."[9] Cyprian wrote to guard the church against schism, a term which for him meant action contrary to the will of the college of bishops.[10] But Cyprian chose familial language to describe such divisions. The church is the family into which we've been born, whether we like our family or not. To name the church as our Mother is to ascribe a familial role to the life of the church, to admit that others within the church are responsible both for our care and for our discipline. (Brown)

In response to the grace of God offered to us in Jesus Christ by the power of the Holy Spirit, we make these vows, these promises. They are promises that recognize our being bound to God and the bonds we have with one another in the church. In the Reformed tradition, baptism functions as what Brown calls the "visible vehicle for incorporation" into the church. In a real sense, the exercise of ordinary discipline does not require us to commit ourselves to any further accountability than the vows we make at baptism.

In Calvin's time and for a long time thereafter, the primary locus of examination of living out these vows was in preparation for coming to the Lord's Table. This was an admirable move, to "discern the body" before communing at the Table. However, in time the system devolved from a mode of discernment to a more technical requirement to have acquired a Communion token to be admitted to the Table. In our day, we must recover the notion of self-examination and corporate discipline around the Table but not in a mechanistic, legalistic fashion. Instead, it must grow out of mutual love, forbearance, and accountability.

One significant worship practice that embodies ordinary discipline is the passing of the peace. More than just a chance to say hello, the passing of the peace in worship gives space for reconciliation. As we noted in chapter 1, this practice of passing the peace is a tangible means of beginning the practice of living peaceably with one another.

It is no mere historical argument that ordinary church discipline is connected to the practices of baptism and the Lord's Supper. One of the grave dangers of the exercise of church discipline is that it can become terrifying—an exercise of power obsessed with mere moralism. We have more than enough examples in the historical record of the overreaching of church discipline to back up this fear. By clearly connecting discipline to the grace offered by God to us in Word and sacrament, we make it more difficult for it to descend into mere moralism. This form of mutual accountability forms us into a community of gratitude.

To be faithful to the Scriptures and to the best of our tradition, we must clearly connect the practice of discipline to the worship life of the church, the hearing of the Word, the engrafting into the church in baptism, and the continual feeding on Christ at the Lord's Table.

MUTUAL CARE AND ACCOUNTABILITY AND THE UNITY OF THE CHURCH

One of the uncomfortable truths of our time is the rampant division in the church. We are baptized into *one* holy catholic and apostolic church, yet after two millennia, says Brown, "the church has (negatively) witnessed innumerable schisms and divisions and has (positively) recognized that appropriate cultural contextualization of the gospel does lead to diversity of thought and practice." We have differences of substance, differences of accent, differences that are kind of hard to explain. The Confession of Belhar calls the unity of the church "a gift and an obligation." As Christina Cleveland argues in her book *Disunity in Christ*, "We need to adopt the belief that to be a follower of Christ means to allow our identity as members of the body of Christ to trump all other identities."[11] Brown believes that "once we name our unity in the Church as our primary identity marker, we start to see that '*to be a follower of Christ* means to care deeply about and pursue other followers of Christ, including ones that we don't instinctively value or like.'"[12]

The Practices of the Upper Room

At the Upper Room, we have lived into this call through the formation of an intimate community whom we often say lives out Romans 12:15:

"Rejoice with those who rejoice; mourn with those who mourn." Worshiping in the round, we see the looks on each other's faces. It's not easy to hide one's joy or one's sorrow in such a context. Our worship services include time for extended sharing of prayer requests, after which congregation members pray for one another, rather than simply having a pastor offer a more priestly pastoral prayer. These were intentional choices to communicate that we belong to one another and that we care for one another as an authentic community. That community then overflows into the preparation of meals for couples with new babies, babysitting for single parents, and other forms of shared congregational care. One Saturday, having received word that a member of the congregation had been hospitalized for seizures, I went to visit her at the local hospital. When I arrived, I found her room already filled with a half-dozen other people from our church.

While celebrating such community, we also remember that we are not sufficient in and of ourselves. The Upper Room's members tend to be in their twenties, thirties, and early forties, and these young adults long for older and wiser voices to speak into their lives. To meet such a need, we formed a creative partnership with another local congregation in which older women from the established church mentor younger women in our congregation. The women of that church—a larger, very wealthy congregation—were delighted to develop a relational partnership in which they were valued for their wisdom, not their finances. Our younger adults in turn benefit from the guidance and relationships they have with other Christians who worship in a very different congregation. With gratitude to the other partner churches who provide financial support of our congregation, I have to say that true mutual care and accountability at the congregation-to-congregation level ought never be separated from genuine relationships.

Authentic relationships are the venue through which God creates the living communion in which mutual care and accountability move beyond obligation and the dead letter of the law into the fullness of Christian love. Anglican missionary, bishop, and theologian John V. Taylor observes in his study of the Holy Spirit titled *The Go-Between God* that "God works always through the moments of recognition when mutual awareness is born."[13] For Taylor, Christian community is participation in a pneumatological reality because the Holy Spirit works "by opening our inward eyes, making us aware of some 'other' beckoning and calling in its separate identity."[14] By beholding the difference of the other while treasuring the gift of communion we receive in Christ, we live into a unity that begets loving care and faithful action. (Brown)

Mutual Care and Accountability
in the Presbyterian Church (U.S.A.)

The practice of mutual care and accountability grows more difficult the further we get away from the local community gathered around Word and sacrament. When corporations are involved (even the nonprofit ones), it is easy for the fiduciary duties to become primary, and the legal system often becomes the place where we resolve things. We end up replacing *mutual* with *adversarial*. And while there are situations that require engagement with the legal system, in many cases it becomes the default so that we can protect ourselves (or our institutions) and not engage in mutual care and accountability. Brown raises this issue in direct relationship to the new worshiping communities movement.

> How can we proclaim that our common baptism into Christ means we still belong to each other in denominational conflicts? If *"mutual care and accountability"* describes not just the local life of a new worshiping community but also the relationship of new worshiping communities and their parent denomination, then the new worshiping communities and their leaders have something significant to contribute to the healing of our denomination. (Brown)

We seem to vacillate between a near idealism and *realpolitik* when it comes to the practices of discipline; we either all sing "Kum Ba Ya" together around the campfire or sue one another in court. From his experience of intimate Christian community, Dietrich Bonhoeffer wrote, "Innumerable times a whole Christian community has broken down because it had sprung from a wish-dream."[15] Rejecting idealism requires all of us, all the parties, to come from a place of humility and to recognize our common bonds in baptism.

Even with these challenges at the national level, Brown sees much occasion for hope. Though mutual accountability may feel fraught at the denominational level, the mutual care that exists between national and local expressions of 1001 New Worshiping Communities offers much to cheer the heart. The Presbyterian Church (U.S.A.) provides generously for the care and nurture of new worshiping communities

and their leaders through grant funding, the development of benefi-
cial resources, hosting conferences, and connecting local leaders with a
national network of trained coaches. And these investments are yield-
ing rich returns. The new worshiping communities that have emerged
in the first few years of the movement differ significantly from traditional and established Presbyterian churches. They are younger, more
ethnically diverse, and much less likely to have participants from Presbyterian backgrounds.[16] These differences alone give new worshiping
communities a prophetic and revitalizing voice within the denomination. Accordingly, increasingly diverse new worshiping communities
may call the church to greater faithfulness in matters of racial justice.
Immigrant fellowships strengthen our bonds to our sisters and brothers in Christ around the globe in places where the church is thriving.
Because the millennial generation values both justice and authentic
spirituality, younger congregations may lead the denomination past
our sad bifurcation of social justice and evangelism.[17] The future of the
church is hopeful.

LIVING AS COMMUNITIES OF GRATITUDE

Mutual care and accountability are expressions of God's grace to us
through the practices of community, through the lives of the saints.
Although such practices are challenging, all those involved in mutual
care and accountability are expressing deep and profound gratitude for
the grace embodied in the practices. Mutual care and accountability
become a fundamental way that a group of people becomes a real community, a community forged by gratitude for the grace offered to us in
Jesus Christ by the power of the Holy Spirit.

9

Communities: Sustainability

And I am sure of this, that he who began a good work in you will bring it to completion at the day of Jesus Christ.

Phil. 1:6

"I wish I had thought about sustainability before the grants ran out," laments one church planter, voicing the concerns of many. An intoxicating rush of energy and enthusiasm marks the early months of a church-planting adventure. Sustained by adrenalin, fair trade coffee, and denominational grants, visionary leaders jump in and do whatever it takes to make a new project fly: setting up folding chairs, passing out flyers, making coffee, walking around neighborhoods, preparing meals, leading Bible studies, playing in a band, or cleaning the bathrooms.

But after a few months or years have gone by, the initial vision fades and people lose their original energy boost and remember other responsibilities to family, home, and jobs. The grant money runs out, and then what?

The issue of sustainability challenges all new worshiping communities. The overseeing church body expects a report that shows exponential growth. Meanwhile the original funding has run low, and the pioneer leaders have moved on to the next exciting project. Every new worshiping community confronts that moment at some point. It marks the time when many trailblazers give up or burn out. What promised to be a fulfilling and inspiring ministry becomes a burden. Leaders wonder if they have the drive for the long haul. Some new communities call it quits. A recent Barna survey indicates that "one-third [of church planters] have considered quitting ministry because of finances, and 35 percent say financial problems cause friction in their marriage."[1] The challenge to sustain a ministry that seems to gobble up endless amounts of energy, time, attention, and money besets every new worshiping community whether it exists in an urban center, a college campus, or a wealthy suburb.

WHAT IS SUSTAINABILITY?

New worshiping communities are not in the institution-building business. Why then discuss sustainability at all? Maybe they really are just idea laboratories, designed as experiments in faith. Perhaps their value to the whole church is inventiveness. New worshiping communities have been called the research and development arm of the church, a blank slate for innovation but not meant to last. In a church locked into stifling traditions, a taste of newness can be intoxicating. Experiments in new forms of church can offer fresh energy to the whole church.

However, drive-by church planting is not the goal for the 1001 New Worshiping Communities initiative either. While our chief end is not to build institutions, we do want to be engaged in Christ's mission, a mission that involves deep, long-term engagement with people, communities, and creation. We seek to embody the character of God who calls us into mission: "Know therefore that the Lord your God is God, the faithful God who maintains covenant loyalty with those who love him and keep his commandments, to a thousand generations" (Deut. 7:9). This is the faithful God we represent.

A New Way of Thinking about Sustainability

Many new worshiping communities form as a response to and in contrast with brittle institutionalism or the perceived irrelevance of established churches. The Presbyterian Church (U.S.A.) has seen the loss of 13 percent of its congregations and over a quarter of its membership in the first fourteen years of the twenty-first century. Most mainline denominations can point to congregations where a handful of elderly members try to maintain drafty old buildings that do not suit the current ministry while maintaining a program more appropriate to a congregation ten times their size. Some older churches survive on the dwindling resources provided by past generations of saints, spending down endowments until eventually the congregation dies out or the building must be sold or catastrophe strikes and the congregation is forced to acknowledge its vulnerability. One elderly elder recently called his presbytery office and left a message: "We quit. Can someone please come and pick up the key to the building."

These images of institutional rigidity and decline have caused the church to seem out of step with the culture. While such churches may have lasted hundreds of years, they do not provide a model for sustainability that resonates with new worshiping communities. Sustainability must mean something brand-new in a movement that is seeking to transform the church.

A New Kind of Church

New worshiping communities launch with a desire to be lithe and nimble, unencumbered by burdens of convention and building, eager to fit a particular cultural context. They embrace slogans like "People before Program" or "Don't Go to Church; Be the Church." They may consist of a small group of people meeting in a living room, coffee shop, street corner, or library. Some of the milestones of maturity in traditional churches, such as erecting a building, calling a pastor, launching a Sunday school program, or running a capital campaign, may not be on the agenda.

For many decades, a commonly accepted church-planting formula called for the purchase of land (preferably twenty acres in a rapidly growing suburb), the construction of a building (well furnished and multipurpose), the hiring of an accomplished staff with a proven track record in church growth, and the launching of a full church program beginning with an attractive worship service. That model of church planting required millions of dollars and imposed harsh financial burdens on newly formed communities as well as their partner congregations. No wonder so many church councils dread embarking on that path again. "We tried it once, and it failed" is a familiar refrain.

What if God has something different in mind than tired old churches and overly ambitious church plants? What if God's vision includes communities worshiping around tables instead of in sanctuaries; worship expressions in a variety of languages and cultural traditions; places where youth and young adults love to hang out and children are always welcome; communities that reflect the rich diversity of God's creation; gatherings where outsiders, artists, and prophets are embraced, and where the church leaves the building and becomes part of the community?

Faithfulness, Not Permanence

This new kind of church requires a different understanding of sustainability. While permanence may not be the goal, long-term faithfulness is. Perhaps the best metaphors for sustainability in new worshiping communities come not from the church world but from the science of ecology. In the world of ecology, sustainable systems are those that see equal resources going into the system as coming out. Sustainable agriculture does not borrow from future generations by robbing the soil of its nutrients today. Sustainable systems are about balance and natural cycles. Diversity is essential to maintaining the resilience needed to adapt to a constantly changing environment. Fairness, rhythm, and strength exist within a sustainable system. In ecology, sustainability is the capacity for endurance. It assumes long life, health, and diversity. A sustainable system should be able to continue indefinitely because no more is coming out of the system than is going into it.

SEEKING SUSTAINABILITY

There is no simple formula for sustainability in this brave new world of twenty-first-century church planting, no one-size-fits-all pathway. Key to the church-planting movement is a commitment to location and particularity. Each new community will grapple with sustainability challenges in its own way. Some will never expect to own buildings. They may be nomadic, trying out a variety of nesting places where the cost is little or nothing. In others, the leaders may be volunteer or bivocational, finding alternative ways to make a living while pouring passion and energy into the new worshiping community. In still other situations, an income-generating activity, such as running a coffee shop or workout center, may supplement the income from offerings. Long-term partnerships with congregations or donors might help other new communities to thrive. Here are some examples of sustainability strategies:

—Union Church runs a coffee and chocolate shop and an event rental venue in downtown Seattle.

—Underwood Park CrossFit in Hudson Falls, New York, serves as both a fitness center and a church.

—The Upper Room in Pittsburgh has two bivocational pastors.

—Hope for Life Chapel in Huntington Beach, California, conducts worship outdoors in an RV park.

—Faithworks: Wings and a Prayer in Paterson, New Jersey, nurtures partnerships with congregations of several denominations.

Three Challenges

While there is no single pathway to sustainability, conversations about sustainability must be woven into the fiber of a new worshiping community, not added on as a patch. There are three basic sustainability challenges for new worshiping communities:

Sustainability of energy

Sustainability of leadership

Sustainability of finances

What we have seen with twenty years of experience in the formation of new pastors through the Company of New Pastors, a pastoral formation program in the Presbyterian Church (U.S.A.), is that technical approaches to sustainability do little good if they are not built on core spiritual practices. Pastors need to be immersed in daily prayer and engagement with Scripture, they need the spiritual support of peers, and they benefit greatly from mentors who have been in their shoes.

Sustainability of Energy

Starting anything from scratch requires boundless stores of energy and focus. It is exciting at first to work as part of a team that pulls together for the greater good of the mission. But the toll on leaders shows up in physical, emotional, and spiritual exhaustion. Depression, burnout, illness, and divorce are common among new worshiping community leaders. Nurturing healthy spiritual practices from the very beginning is essential to long-term sustainability. Modeling the practices of Sabbath, prayer, retreat, and rhythms of life becomes part of the purpose of the community. Communities that last develop a rule of life that sustains the community itself and its participants. They try not to do more than they can realistically accomplish.

Healthy practices provide an antidote to the stresses of the contemporary society. Many new worshiping communities choose not to produce church programs, opting instead to spend time and attention on community listening and relationship building. Appropriate times spent in rest and renewal balance the hard work of starting a new community and nurture the body and soul. Incorporating spiritual disciplines into the core ministry of a new worshiping community is life giving. There is a renewed interest in ancient practices such as Sabbath keeping and simplicity. The Fourth Commandment takes on new importance:

> Remember the Sabbath day, and keep it holy. Six days you shall labor and do all your work. But the seventh day is a Sabbath to the Lord your God; you shall not do any work—you, your son or your daughter, your male or female slave, your livestock, or the alien resident in your towns. For in six days the Lord made heaven and earth, the sea, and all that is in them, but rested the seventh day; therefore the Lord blessed the Sabbath day and consecrated it." (Deut. 20:8–11)

The Open Door in Pittsburgh has developed a "rule of life" for its members that honors the primacy of God in the life of the community. Here is a section of it:

Community Practices

We seek to live in the way of Jesus by practicing simple weekly rhythms—to regularly

Listen to God

We seek to practice listening by setting aside at least 1 focused time of listening to God's "still, small voice" each week. . . .

Learn from God

We seek to practice learning by devoting at least 1 focused time of learning, from Christ, through scripture each week. . . .

Eat with others

We strive to eat with at least 2 people we don't live with (1 from the Open Door and 1 not) each week. . . .

Encourage others

We seek to practice encouragement by intentionally encouraging 2 people through words, gifts or actions each week. . . .

Give ourselves away to the world

We look for regular ways to give away our time, money, skills and/ or passions to others and the world.[2]

Sustainability of Leadership

Sustainability without appropriate leadership is impossible. At the start, many new worshiping communities fall under the authority of the session of an established congregation or a committee of the presbytery. This kind of nurturing can provide the safety net needed for the new community to launch, but if the core leadership doesn't come as quickly as possible from the community itself, the project is unlikely to last for the long haul. A new worshiping community in a trailer park needs trailer park residents on the leadership team. A collegiate community needs leaders who are college students. This principle challenges a key assumption of the Presbyterian Church (U.S.A.) that the leader of any worshiping community must be previously equipped for church leadership by going to seminary, passing exams, and showing "success" in ministry.

While 55 percent of the leaders of new worshiping communities are teaching elders of the Presbyterian Church (U.S.A.), the remainder reflect a new kind of leadership that God is preparing for the harvest. Some are ruling elders, some are ordained by partner denominations in other countries, and some have had very little leadership experience in the traditional church.[3] The Fresh Expressions movement in the United Kingdom has found that most of its leaders have had no previous leadership experience in the church.[4] There has been a shift away from looking for people who have the credentials to serve as church leaders and fitting them into positions of leadership to observing who is providing spiritual leadership and helping those persons attain the training and authorization needed for the ministry.

Local leadership is essential to the sustainability of a new worshiping community. Jeremiah's instructions to the Israelite people living in enemy territory provide some guidance: "Build houses and live in them; plant gardens and eat what they produce. . . . Multiply there, and do not decrease. But seek the welfare of the city where I have sent you into exile, and pray to the Lord on its behalf, for in its welfare you will find your welfare" (Jer. 29:5–7). In much the same way, twenty-first-century church planters put down roots in a community and lead from a deep love and understanding of a particular context. They serve as shalom-bearers to the neighborhood.

Sustainability of Finances

Although sustainability is about more than money, one cannot think seriously about sustainability without talking about money, an uncomfortable subject for many church leaders. Some people feel threatened or shamed when church leaders broach the topic of money. Often the conversation about money recalls painful childhood memories. The "dechurched" or "dones" (as in "Been there, tried that, done with church") may particularly remember shame or hurt connected with money requests from churches of their past.

However, Jesus talked about money a lot. Christ followers take up the call to discipleship when they follow him down that rocky road. Those who do discover rich rewards. On first blush, talking about money in church just seems wrong. After all, church is all about spiritual things, and money just seems so unspiritual. Jesus often juxtaposes spiritual things and worldly things such as money, and worldly things always come out the losers. This might cause one to decide that the most spiritual approach is to avoid the money talk altogether. Too many church planters choose that route and realize too late that avoiding the hard conversation may be blocking the opportunity for spiritual growth among the participants and denying the long-term sustainability of the community.

Why did Jesus have so much to say about money? Perhaps it was because he knew that the only way to fulfillment, joy, and peace is to put God first in our lives. The most common obstacles to putting God first are money and the things money can buy. Therefore, money is a spiritual issue. How we relate to money and the things money can buy says a lot about our discipleship.

Healthy ministry finances are marked by transparency and focus on the mission. Scott Mackenzie has written a compelling book (with a cheesy subtitle) about the ministry of giving: *Bounty: Ten Ways to Increase Giving at Your Church*. Mackenzie suggests that community leaders be completely open about their own stewardship and that the testimony of those who have learned the blessing of giving call others into supporting mission. Mackenzie's challenge to pastors to tell their congregations exactly how much they give to the congregation's mission is bracing but refreshing.[5] Consideration of finances can become integral to the mission of the community, not a necessary evil for sustainability.

If we go into this new kind of ministry understanding that our goal is to make disciples, we take seriously the job of helping new disciples walk in the way of Jesus. Jesus sent his disciples out on the road without sandals, bags, or a change of clothes, all burdens that can get in the way of putting Jesus first.

CHURCH PLANTING IN VULNERABLE COMMUNITIES

After decades of thinking that new church development must happen in affluent suburbs, Presbyterians are finding that new worshiping communities are springing up among the most vulnerable of God's children in homeless shelters, on street corners, on college campuses, in immigrant farming communities, and in trailer parks. This kind of contextual church planting brings on its own challenges to financial sustainability.

Those who contribute financially to the health and growth of the ministry find ownership and belonging, even if the contribution is small. Giving generously is a spiritual discipline that enables disciples to put God first in their own lives. While grants may be necessary for helping to jump-start a new ministry, local ownership of finance and strategy are the route to long-term sustainability.

One new worshiping community is in a poor urban neighborhood besieged by crime, drugs, homelessness, and unemployment. Worship services are held on Friday evening on the street corner where sex workers and drug dealers conduct business and where rival gangs battle over territory. At one service, the worship leaders chose not to pass the offering plate to avoid pressuring or embarrassing the humble congregation. At the end of the service, one man dressed in tattered clothing waved a couple of crumpled dollar bills in his hand (perhaps all he owned) and said, "Where's the offering plate? I brought my offering." Clearly it was important for this worshiper to contribute his mite.

TEACHING STEWARDSHIP

Sara Hayden works as associate for the Southeast Region for the 1001 New Worshiping Communities initiative. She grew up in a church plant started by her parents and remains deeply committed to the transformative work of missional church planting. She has this to say about the role of stewardship in new worshiping communities:

> When a project or leader approaches a national church or a funding partner with the expectation that the partner will fund something that the leader and community are themselves unwilling to fund, the result more commonly reflects the adage "If you want advice, ask for money." In this mixed economy of church (that meets people where they are in a particular community but also transforms), leaders need start-up funding, but they also need a budget that is ultimately locally raised and based on an awareness of the local economy.[6]
>
> The missional church does not teach stewardship in order to float its budget for ministry that has not yet occurred. The church teaches stewardship as a way of life because stewardship is *formational* for the steward and, ultimately, is a witness to the community to which we are sent and with whom we are called to partner. This takes time. But in communities that are awakening or reawakening to God, almost nothing can be more important than realizing that one's life, and all its assets, is a gift. The most important thing about stewardship—and the gospel, come to think of it—is not what it does *for* us but what it does *to* us. (Hayden)

MATURE EXPRESSIONS OF CHURCH

New worshiping communities aim to become mature expressions of church in their own right, not "church-lite," or bridges to "real" church, or one more program in an established congregation. Their expression of church is unique and appropriate to their particular neighborhoods. New worshiping communities have an essential ecclesiology in their DNA. Like young children, they grow to maturity. A mature expression of church includes a grown-up look at the power and the challenge of seeing money as one of the resources that God provides in abundance to those who place their trust in God alone.

At their best, new worshiping communities engage in giving that is both rigorously faithful and freeing. It is *they and their community partners*, not a midcouncil budget or a grant system, that determines the budget that ultimately works for them in their context. Whether the annual budget is five thousand or half a million dollars, faithful stewardship requires sacrificial giving, first and foremost, by the leadership team, *including paid staff.* The point of the missional new worshiping community is to serve as a witness of God's call to all people. We should not measure the success of a new worshiping community by the ability of a group of people to raise an amount of money that a specific socioeconomic demographic historically budgeted for its church. Success, ultimately, should be measured by the contemporary witness of a group of people who are called and sent to be ambassadors of God's grace in the world. This does, of course, necessitate a faithful grappling of resources and a sacrificial giving toward the corporate good. But it is this faithful exercise of stewardship, not the amount of the budget itself, that bears fruit and witness.

If you are worried about the budget of your church, start giving. If you are not willing to give, ask yourself: Why would anyone else? Local partners of the church—secular businesses, schools, partner churches, fellow entrepreneurs—follow a witness where treasure and heart are aligned.

If *fruitfulness* is the Bible's term for success, then the fruitful next church ultimately produces transformed people going out to be the witnesses of God to a world that is both hungry and overfed. It looks like a community taking God's story seriously enough to live it out when the worshiping gathering ends. (Hayden)

Achieving sustainability for new worshiping communities involves a long and challenging journey. It requires attention to the whole picture of sustainability, including energy, leadership, and finances. It is an expression of faithfulness. It is part of the maturation of the new community and requires the participation of the whole community. Every new community struggles with challenges of sustainability. Some decide that the challenge is too hard and end up quitting prematurely. Those who take on the challenge find rich reward in growing deeper in spiritual practices and faithfulness.

10

The Future of New Worshiping Communities

The 2012 launch of the 1001 New Worshiping Communities initiative was a grand gesture greeted with energy and enthusiasm. At a time when discouragement and conflict ran rampant in the church and when the faithful yearned for a word of hope, the 1001 initiative caught the imagination of the denomination and was noted around the world. There was evidence that the Holy Spirit was up to something and that the church had a future, albeit a different one than most members had anticipated. Celebration and cautious optimism were the order of the day.

Much has been learned since then, and there still remains much to be learned. That is the focus of this final chapter. While there is much to celebrate in the launch of new communities, there are no easy answers or quick fixes to the challenges facing the whole church. There is much the wider church can learn from new worshiping communities. We will explore both the opportunities that the movement has introduced to the dynamic of church vitality and the unique challenges new worshiping communities present.

WHAT'S GOING ON?

When the 1001 New Worshiping Communities initiative launched, a ten-year longitudinal research project also began tracking the progress of the movement and keeping the church accountable to its goals.

Many of the trends and statistics from this chapter owe their existence to the diligent sociologists and statisticians in the Research Services of the Presbyterian Church (U.S.A.) who have tracked almost every facet of new worshiping communities. The objectives of the research project have been defined this way:

> There are three main objectives to this research. First is to track the progress of the 1001 New Worshiping Communities initiative—how many communities are being generated, what do they look like, and how are they operating? Second is to track awareness of the initiative within (mid-councils), and among . . . members, teaching elders, and ruling elders. Third is to determine the level of success of the new communities themselves—are they thriving, what is working for them, and what do they still need in order to better grow in their mission?[1]

We recognize that statistics and reports tell only a part of any story. The most important part involves transformed lives and reconciled relationships. We recommend looking at the Presbyterian Mission website for a series of videos that flesh out the narrative that this chapter outlines in numbers and percentages.[2]

WHAT HAVE WE LEARNED?

Each community yields its own lessons, and a detailed analysis of each project could be a book in itself. We have drawn some themes and generalities from the stories and statistics. In this chapter, we will address the following themes:

New worshiping communities enhance the diversity of the church

New worshiping communities reach younger people

New worshiping communities experiment with new forms of church

New worshiping communities reach unchurched and dechurched people

New worshiping communities face sustainability challenges

New Worshiping Communities Enhance Diversity

An adage acknowledges that the Presbyterian Church (U.S.A.) is older, richer, and whiter than the nation. Despite decades of strategies and action plans designed to increase the diversity of the denomination, the PC(USA) hovers around the 9 percent mark when it comes to participation by people of color. The 1001 initiative has turned that figure upside down right from the beginning. The latest research shows that 46 percent of new worshiping community participants are people of color. New worshiping communities engage new immigrants, refugees, and second-generation Koreans and Latinx in ways the traditional church has failed to do. Sixteen percent of the participants are Hispanic or Latinx, 12 percent are Asian, 11 percent are African immigrants, and 2 percent are Middle Eastern. Interestingly, only 1 percent of new worshiping community participants are African American, compared to 4 percent of organized church members.[3]

The leadership statistics are similar. While 88 percent of PC(USA) pastors are white, only 60 percent of new worshiping community leaders are white. Meanwhile, 12 percent of the leaders identify as Asian, 11 percent as Hispanic or Latinx, 9 percent as African immigrant, 4 percent as African American, and 4 percent as mixed race.[4] Another interesting statistic about leadership for new worshiping communities is that 40 percent of the leaders are not Presbyterian-ordained teaching elders. Some are ruling elders (sometimes commissioned by a presbytery for their service), ordained in another denomination, or not ordained at all.[5] The movement is calling and equipping a new leadership cohort for the denomination and for the wider church.

Twenty-nine percent of the participants in new worshiping communities primarily speak a language other than English. While, expectedly, the largest number of non-English speakers converse in Spanish (9 percent) or Korean (6 percent), there are communities that worship in Arabic, Ewe, Kiswahili, Tagalog, Tamil, and Twi, all languages for which the PC(USA) has little ability to provide support resources.[6] This presents challenges as the denomination seeks to prepare coaches and provide assessments, training, and print resources in a variety of languages. Not only translation is required (which is challenging enough) but also a deep understanding of cultural traditions and values.

These statistics of diversity are exciting and bring hope to a denomination that has promoted racial and ethnic equality without demonstrating much skill in achieving its ends. The pictures of new worshiping communities convey a very different image of the church of the future. What impact will this have on the wider church? More research is needed to determine the extent of the influence, but there are a few hints: "Leaders of color are more likely to emphasize evangelism: 30% of leaders of color list evangelism as one of their top three priorities, compared to only 8% of white leaders. Additionally, leaders of color are more likely than white [leaders] to use testimonial evangelism."[7] Testimonial evangelism is defined as "sharing the Good News and telling your God story."[8] It will be interesting to see what impact this "God story" will have on the church of the future.

New Worshiping Communities Reach Younger People

The Presbyterian Church (U.S.A.) and most other mainline denominations have struggled to reach the millennial generation. The median age of a Presbyterian has inched upward to its current point of sixty-two. Would new worshiping communities buck this trend? This question was on the minds of those who proposed the new initiative in 2012. For decades, church members have lamented the loss of young people in the pews. According to Perry Chang, research associate for the Presbyterian Church (U.S.A.), each younger birth cohort, across all denominational groups, is less likely to be involved in church than the one before it, and the percentage of religious "nones" (those who claim no religious affiliation) has been growing in the United States since 1990. Could this be a turning point for the church?

The initial news is hopeful. According to the research study, "60% of new worshiping community participants are aged 13-45, compared to 47% of members of PC(USA) congregations."[9] New communities thrive on college campuses and even in high schools. Almost three-quarters of Presbyterian new worshiping communities indicate that their mission focuses on engaging youth, young adults, or college students.

While not all new worshiping communities include young people, the overall age skews significantly lower than that of the average Presbyterian church: "NWC participants tend to be younger than PC(USA) members as a whole. The largest age group in PC(USA) congregations is over 65. In contrast, the largest age group within NWCs is 26-45. This indicates that NWCs are attracting younger participants."[10] A 2015 study indicates that 64 percent of the participants in new worshiping communities are under the age of 40.[11]

We do not yet have the research to show why new worshiping communities appeal to a younger audience than traditional churches do. However, informal surveys and conversations show that the authenticity of the relationships, the informality of the gatherings, the hospitality toward unchurched people, the openness to questioning of traditional faith tenets, and the flexibility in worship times and locations all contribute. Many young adults applaud the acting out of faith through involvement in social justice and compassion ministries. While there is much yet to study, there seem to be things the established church can learn from new worshiping communities if it is truly committed to engaging younger people.

New Worshiping Communities Explore New Forms of Church

The assumption that starting a new worshiping community begins with a building and a worship service has been the most obvious upset of the 1001 initiative. With groups of people forming faith communities in bars or gyms or boats, the sky has become the limit—quite literally, as several of the new communities meet in the open air.

Exploring new forms of worship involves questioning many church traditions. When and where do worship gatherings happen to best engage the intended community? How is the gospel proclaimed to people without a tradition of church attendance? How will the sacraments be celebrated? What is the starting point for forming community?

While 48 percent of new worshiping communities meet in a building owned by a church, it is also true that 21 percent meet in homes, 27 percent meet in coffee shops or bars, and 8 percent meet outdoors.[12] Most that meet in a church building are using free or rental space offered by another congregation. Building ownership is seldom on the radar screen of a new worshiping community, and in the rare situations when a community acquires property, the building usually serves multiple purposes and lacks the traditional accoutrements of church architecture.

In a neighborhood where twelve closed churches had been turned into bars, the Hot Metal Bridge Faith Community in Pittsburgh bought a bar and turned it into a church. Missing Peace in Ormond, Florida, has a variety of meeting places. Depending on the focus of their worship experience for that day, you may find them at the beach, in a museum, in an old church building, or at a member's home. Union Church in Seattle meets in a space they own that doubles as a coffee and chocolate shop, rental venue for weddings or parties, and a homeless shelter. Mision Presbiteriana Rio Grande in Puerto Rico meets in a tiny storefront space but takes worship to people in public housing projects and in a city park.

Fifty-one percent of the communities surveyed describe their worship style as "non-traditional."[13] While that can be a generic term, some leaders of new worshiping communities shared what they mean by nontraditional in the following ways:

— "We gather in a cafe, around round tables, instead of pews. It is also an open format since a majority have never been in church before, they are able to ask questions during the presentation of the Word."

— "Sermons can be interactive. Prayer of Confession is often a manual activity. There is movement in the service, and we try to be multisensory with the worship service."

— "We rotate through different worship styles honoring the physical, cerebral, spiritual, and service in turn."

— "Most of the folks we work with have been turned away from the church and so the way in has been through nontraditional worship. We have no bulletins, and everything we do is sung."

— "The emphasis is on vulnerability and deep sharing of life across boundaries."

— "Worship is participatory, involving many voices reading prayers and adding to the message."[14]

When researchers asked about the activities of new worshiping communities, they learned the following: "Overall, leaders rate building relationships, worshiping, and disciple-making as the most important activities. . . . In the interviews [part of the research project], many leaders refer to this combined emphasis as incarnational ministry— expressed as leaving the building, Jesus among the people, taking Jesus to the streets, meeting people where they are, etc. 'As people of Christ, we are called not only to come, but also to go.'"[15]

New Worshiping Communities Reach the UnChurched and Dechurched

When the new worshiping communities movement began, one of its key objectives was to find a way of making new disciples of Christ. Adult baptisms have become increasingly rare in the Presbyterian Church, with most new members joining a church through a letter of

transfer or reaffirmation of faith (which themselves are on the decline).
It felt like a risk to put the goal of making new disciples right up there
in the definition of a new worshiping community. Discussions about
evangelism were difficult for Presbyterians. The word *evangelical* had
taken on an identity of its own that felt uncomfortable to many mainline Protestants. This discomfort only increased when friction on the
political front caused *evangelical Christian* to became associated with
specific political positions.

But the 1001 initiative took on the challenge of making new disciples
without any clear plan for how this would happen. Despite our lack of
experience or toolkit, the 1001 initiative has been meeting its goals.
For 42 percent of the participants in new worshiping communities,
going to church is a new experience. This includes the 12 percent who
did not have a previous faith affiliation, the 9 percent who came from
a non-Christian faith, and the 21 percent who describe themselves as
dechurched (defined as not having attended church within the last five
years). Only 20 percent previously attended a PC(USA) congregation.[16]

The research shows that one of the strongest differences between
new worshiping communities and established congregations is the
form of evangelism used:

> The most common style of evangelism used by NWCs is invitational,
> followed by missional and relational; however, only 31% of congrega-
> tions make frequent use of relational evangelism, compared to 77% of
> NWCs. There is also a large gap between NWCs and congregations
> in the use of testimonial evangelism; this is particularly interesting,
> given that sharing the Good News and telling your "God story" is
> a more traditional style of evangelism, but is used by the more non-
> traditional NWCs (although it is the style they use the least, still
> over half of NWCs engage in testimonial evangelism). In fact, aside
> from missional evangelism (where there is no significant difference),
> NWCs are more likely than congregations to frequently engage in
> all five listed styles of evangelism. Quite simply, NWCs report doing
> more evangelism, and in more ways, than do congregations.[17]

New Worshiping Communities Struggle with Sustainability

Of the approximately 460 new worshiping communities started since
2012 as part of the 1001 initiative, sixty no longer show up on the
active list. While the numbers can be misleading because some of the

sixty thrive despite no longer identifying with the movement, a fair number of projects will not grow to maturity. We expect this in a movement characterized by experimentation. Any research and development department will attest that not all experiments lead to a finished product. But it does cause us to pause and explore what makes some of the experiments bear long-term fruit while others remain in the realm of important experiments. There is much to learn from the new communities that continue to grow and flourish and more still to learn from those that fall short of their own expectations.

The leadership team of the 1001 initiative has begun to study the communities that have closed prematurely. We are learning that each community that reaches the end of its life does so for a different reason or combination of reasons, although we can pick out some common threads. Here are some of the factors that lead to prolonged sustainability:

> Support from the broader church
>
> Clear vision
>
> Sustainability strategy
>
> Right leader in place

Support from the Broader Church

Support from the broader church provides a safety net in the early years when new communities struggle the most. The support needed is not just financial, although financial needs are significant for a new ministry. New worshiping community leaders may show extraordinary gifts for evangelism, disciple-making, worship leadership, and outreach without knowing how to raise funds, hire staff, or develop a financial plan. They may not have identified a space to hold meetings or worship services. They may lack knowledge of church governance and administrative policies. The broader church may possess some skills that the new community needs. Beyond specific skills, the new community needs recognition, authorization, and oversight. Without this care and accountability, the new worshiping community remains vulnerable and off the radar screen of the larger church.

Some midcouncils have a clear vision for starting new worshiping communities and have developed support structures. Some are inexperienced or lacking in resources and are poorly equipped to support new worshiping communities. A few are actively resistant to new worshiping communities. There is work to be done in helping midcouncils and thriving congregations develop the skills to provide the primary support system for new communities.

Clear Vision

Another reason for premature closure can be the lack of a clearly articulated vision that is accepted by everyone on the team. In their defense, new worshiping community leaders tend to be pioneers who have no qualms about stepping out into new territory without a map. Their willingness to take risks and travel a new path are essential to their role as new worshiping community leaders. However, with the wagon train in tow, a map helps keep the focus honed in on the main objective. New worshiping communities often jump into the fray without a game plan. The focus of the communities can quickly shift from vision to sustainability if the vision is not clearly articulated and accepted by the participants. When they disintegrate, we often hear that different groups held different expectations. This confusion may lead to disappointment and conflict. (The denominational support resource *Starting New Worshiping Communities* is designed to help walk leadership teams through the discernment process that leads to a clear vision.[18])

Sustainability Strategy

"There's just so much *nothing* at the start," explained one new worshiping community leader. When asked to expand, he pointed out the lack of a building, staff, Bibles, leaders, chairs, hymnals, Sunday school curriculum, coffee pot, computer, projector, musical instruments, meeting space, website—the list goes on.

What is the route from "so much nothing" to a mature expression of church? That question is addressed in much more detail in chapter 9, but in summary, many new worshiping communities fail to think about long-term sustainability until the initial funding from denominational sources or individual supporters begins to run out.

There is no single strategy for sustainability in contextual church planting. The plan is integrally connected to the context. However, in every context, sustainability matters and needs to be defined at the outset. In our experience, this may be the most commonly overlooked part of vision-casting in new worshiping communities.

Having a solid relationship of care and accountability with a mid-council or congregation can help to prepare for the future. New worshiping communities have often been compared to children who need the support, care, love, and discipline of a loving community at first but are on the pathway toward maturity. One of the marks of maturity is taking gradual ownership of finances. Another piece of the support system comes from a coach who can help the new community anticipate the challenges ahead and prepare for them.

Right Leader in Place

A fourth reason that the vision may not succeed is that the wrong leader is in place. The innovative work of starting a new worshiping community is not for everyone. There is no template for the ideal new worshiping community leader because all communities are contextual, and the right leader for a community of graduate students in the Northeast may fail miserably in a church made up of Texas ranchers or West Coast techies. However, there are some clear markers of the temperament of successful church planters.

Deep Faith. New worshiping community leaders have a firm faith in the triune God, with grounded spiritual practices to back it up. They are able to tell their faith story in a way that is both engaging and compelling. God is more than an abstract concept; God is a tangible reality. There are many pitfalls and challenges along the road of church planting. Some church authorities misunderstand the work of starting new worshiping communities. The leaders may face criticism and discouragement. It can be lonely work with little to show in the early days. Faith that this work is God's calling is essential, and daily contact with God sustains the leader through challenging times. But the leader's faith is not just a personal experience; he or she is part of a community that provides support, nurture, and accountability.

Innovative Spirit. New worshiping community leaders have an innovative spirit. Has the leader ever started something new? What process did he follow? Who did she gather around her? How did she communicate the vision and keep everyone on the same team? There are people who seem born to start new ventures. This gift combines the generation of new ideas with the discipline, hard work, and planning to take the idea to fruition. Michael Moynagh of Fresh Expressions in the

U.K. says this about innovation: "Innovation is the modification of the 'rules of the game' so that church develops in new ways."[19] He stresses that innovation is not incompatible with tradition. In fact, he says, the church has always innovated at the same time it has passed along the faith of the past. He concludes that "innovation is foundational to Christian inheritance."[20]

At a time when the culture is changing so rapidly, the spiritual gift of innovation is needed more than ever. The leader without an innovative spirit can easily succumb to maintenance ministry. Creativity reflects the image of a creator God and is a key component of new worshiping community leadership.

Social Base. Church planting is taxing on energy and relationships. The leaders who are in the work for the long haul have a strong social base of family and friends, mentors, colleagues, and coaches who support what they are doing and help to keep them accountable. A strong support system ensures appropriate boundaries, provides honest feedback, and offers encouragement at times of stress.

Connections with Unchurched People. Many church people find all of their friends and social contacts within the church. In fact, some cannot name a single person important to their life who does not go to church somewhere. New worshiping community leaders enjoy nurturing friendships outside the church. They have relationships of mutuality and trust within the wider community and feel comfortable living as people of faith within a circle of people who question or reject Christianity. They can point to examples of friendships they have nurtured with people who are different from themselves. Building new relationships and conducting mutually respectful conversations about faith with non-Christians feels exciting and energizing to new worshiping community leaders.

Flexibility and Resilience. There are plenty of ups and downs in the work of starting a new worshiping community. A person with flexibility and resilience commits to a course of action to accomplish a long-range goal, stays engaged over a long period of time despite setbacks, plans ahead, and maintains perseverance and passion for long-term goals.

An assessment is the best way to find out if church planting is the right fit. For those with the right package of skills, practices, and calling, it can be the most satisfying ministry in the world.

WHERE ARE WE GOING?

The original vision for 1001 New Worshiping Communities alluded to its potential to help with the transformation of the whole church. The assumption is that a church in need of change needs room to experiment and try new things. While our established churches leave very little leeway for experimentation, new worshiping communities provide a laboratory for trial and error.

We can see from the data that many of our hopes are being borne out. This is good news.

As the church moves into its God-given future fueled by the hope we have in Christ Jesus, it has much to learn from the risky, experimental, hope-filled work of the pioneers who have started new worshiping communities. As the movement continues to grow, it provides a laboratory for research on the ways the church can do things differently in its attempts to engage unchurched people, make new disciples, and continue in its long journey of faithfulness.

However, we must reiterate the theological convictions that we started this book with. This experimentation will be truly of God when it is based on the hope of the gospel, a hope that is rooted in the grace of our Lord Jesus Christ. It will show forth good fruit only insofar as it is infused with the sustaining power of the Holy Spirit. These new communities of gratitude will flourish when they embody the love of God to all in their contexts. Should this happen, then the 1001 New Worshiping Communities may indeed kindle faith, revitalize communities, and possibly even contribute to the ongoing life of that part of the people of God called the Presbyterian Church (U.S.A.).

Notes

1. Communities of Grace and Gratitude

1. Church of Scotland, *Book of Common Order*, 2nd ed. (Edinburgh: Saint Andrew Press, 1996), 83.

2. Karl Barth, *Church Dogmatics*, IV.1.2 (Edinburgh: T. & T. Clark, 1960), para. 57.2.

3. *The Constitution of the Presbyterian Church (U.S.A.)*, Part I, *Book of Confessions* (Louisville, KY: Office of the General Assembly, 2016), 4.086.

4. Augustine, "Homily on the Epistle of John, VII," in *Nicene and Post-Nicene Fathers*, vol. 7, ed. Philip Schaff (Peabody, MA: Hendrickson, 1995), para. 8.

5. *Book of Confessions*, 7.251.

6. *The Constitution of the Presbyterian Church (U.S.A.)*, Part II, *Book of Order* (Louisville, KY: Office of the General Assembly, 2016), F-1.0301.

2. NEW: What's New in New Worshiping Communities?

1. *Mission-Shaped Church: Church Planting and Fresh Expressions of Church in a Changing Context* (London: Church House Publishing, 2004), 11.

2. Ibid, 13.

3. Ibid, 34.

4. Michael Moynagh, *Church in Life: Innovation, Mission, and Ecclesiology* (London: SCM Press, 2017), 10.

5. 1001 New Worshiping Communities, "Presbyteries Receive Inspiration and Energy," https://www.youtube.com/watch?v=oU1cMOysGE8&t=28s.

3. New: Forming New Disciples

1. James Walker, *Dirty Word: The Vulgar, Offensive Language of the Kingdom of God* (Nashville: Discipleship Resources, 2008), 20.

2. Frank Newport, "More Than 9 in 10 Americans Continue to Believe in God," Gallup report, http://www.gallup.com/poll/147887/americans-continue -believe-god.aspx.

3. Tom Clegg and Warren Bird, *Lost in America: How You and Your Church Can Impact the World Next Door* (Loveland, CO: Group Publishing, 2001), 25.

4. Madeline L'Engle, *Walking on Water: Reflections on Faith and Art* (Colorado Springs, CO: Waterbrook Press, 2001), 113.

5. *1001 NWC Leaders Report*, February 2017, PC(USA) Research Services report, 14.

6. Karl Barth, *Deliverance to the Captives* (New York: Harper Brothers, 1961), 75–84.

7. Diana Butler Bass, *Christianity after Religion: The End of Church and the Birth of a New Spiritual Awakening* (New York: HarperCollins, 2012), 205.

8. John Calvin, *Institutes of the Christian Religion* 3.2.7; ed. John McNeil, trans. Ford Lewis Battles (Philadelphia: Westminster Press, 1960), 1:551.

9. Eugene H. Peterson, *A Long Obedience in the Same Direction: Discipleship in an Instant Society* (Downers Grove, IL: InterVarsity Press, 2000).

4. New: Forms of Church

1. Stated Clerk, *Minutes of the General Assembly of the Presbyterian Church in the United States of America*, New Series Vol I (New York: Presbyterian Board of Publications, 1870), 119.

2. Michael Frost and Alan Hirsch, *The Shaping of Things to Come: Innovation and Mission for the 21st-Century Church*, rev. and updated ed. (Grand Rapids, MI: Baker Books, 2013); Alan Hirsch, *The Forgotten Ways: Reactivating the Missional Church* (Grand Rapids, MI: Brazos Press, 2006).

3. George G. Hunter, *How to Reach Secular People* (Nashville: Abingdon Press, 1992); Thom S. Rainer and Eric Geiger, *Simple Church: Returning to God's Process for Making Disciples* (Nashville: Broadman Press, 2006).

4. Milfred Minatrea, *Shaped by God's Heart: The Passion and Practices of Missional Churches* (San Francisco: Jossey-Bass, 2004); Reggie McNeal, *Missional Communities: The Rise of the Post-Congregational Church* (San Francisco: Jossey-Bass, 2011); Jonathan Wilson-Hartgrove, *New Monasticism: What It Has to Say to Today's Church* (Grand Rapids, MI: Brazos Press, 2008).

5. Presbyterian Mission Agency, "What Is a New Worshiping Community?" http://www.onethousandone.org/#!define-new-worship-comm/c235g.

6. David Bosch suggests "action in hope" as one paradigm for mission. David Jacobus Bosch, *Transforming Mission: Paradigm Shifts in Theology of Mission*, vol. 16 (Maryknoll, NY: Orbis Books, 1991), 510.

7. 1001 New Worshiping Communities, "East End Fellowship," https://www.youtube.com/watch?v=BBcrJVbPpMY.

5. WORSHIPING

1. Darrell Guder, "Missional Center of Reformed Worship," *Reformed Liturgy and Worship* 32, no. 2 (1998): 101.

2. Ibid., 100.

3. A. D. Miller, quoted in Jean-Jacques von Allmen, *Worship: Its Theology and Practice* (New York: Oxford University Press, 1965), 52.

4. Guder, "Missional Center," 101.

5. Ibid.

6. Ibid.

7. *The Constitution of the Presbyterian Church (U.S.A.)*, Part II, *Book of Order* (Louisville, KY: Office of the General Assembly, 2015), W-2.0202.

8. Guder, "Missional Center," 102.

9. See "Accompanying Letter to the Confession of Belhar," in *The Constitution of the Presbyterian Church (U.S.A.)*, Part I, *Book of Confessions* (Louisville, KY: Office of the General Assembly, 2016), 305–6.

10. *1001 NWC Leaders' Report*, February 2017, PC(USA) Research Services report, http://www.presbyterianmission.org/wp-content/uploads/1001-NWC-final-report-with-appendices.pdf, 21.

11. Ibid., 24.

6. Worshiping: Word and Sacrament

1. John Calvin, *Institutes of the Christian Religion* 4.1.9; ed. John McNeil, trans. Ford Lewis Battles (Philadelphia: Westminster Press, 1960), 2:1023.

2. See ibid., 4.1.1: "I shall start, then, with the church, into whose bosom God is pleased to gather his sons, not only that they may be nourished by her help and ministry as long as they are infants and children, but also that they may be guided by her motherly care until they mature and at last reach the goal of faith."

3. See *The Constitution of the Presbyterian Church (U.S.A.)*, Part I, *Book of Confessions* (Louisville, KY: Office of the General Assembly, 2016), 3.18.

4. Ibid., 4.1.8.

5. Ibid., 4.1.9.

6. Ibid.

7. Emile Léonard, *A History of Protestantism*, vol. 2 (London: Nelson, 1965), 103.

8. John Calvin, "To the Believers in the Isles" in *Letters of John Calvin*, trans. Jules Bonnet (New York: B. Franklin, 1972), 2:432.

9. Léonard, *History of Protestantism*, 103–4.

10. John Calvin, "To the Brethren of Poitou," in *Letters of John Calvin*, trans. Jules Bonnet (New York: B. Franklin, 1972), 3:44.

11. *The Constitution of the Presbyterian Church*, Part II, *Book of Order* (Louisville, KY: Office of the General Assembly, 2015), W-3.0409.

12. See Charles Wiley, *Ordinary and Extraordinary Discipline: Mutual Accountability in the Reformed Tradition* (Louisville, KY: Office of Theology and Worship, 2002).

13. Directory for Worship, W-3.0403, 3.0410.

7. Worshiping: Sent by the Spirit

1. Stanley Hauerwas, *Resident Aliens: Life in the Christian Colony*, expanded 25th anniversary ed. (Nashville: Abingdon Press, 2014), 101.

2. Ibid.

3. Ibid., 102.

4. Catherine Mowry LaCugna, *God for Us: The Trinity and Christian Life* (San Francisco: HarperSanFrancisco, 1993), ix.

5. David Bosch, *Transforming Mission* (Maryknoll, NY: Orbis, 1994), 390.

6. Libby Tedder Hugus, "Prayer and Our Relationship with God," in *Relational Theology: A Contemporary Introduction*, ed. Brint Montgomery, Thomas J. Ord, and Karen Strand Winslow (San Diego: Point Loma Press, 2012), loc. 1004, Kindle.

7. Christopher J. H. Wright, *The Mission of God's People: A Biblical Theology of the Church's Mission* (Grand Rapids, MI: Zondervan, 2011), 26–27.

8. Lausanne Committee for World Evangelization, "The Lausanne Covenant," 1974, http://www.lausanne.org/covenant.

8. COMMUNITIES of Care and Accountability

1. Stefan Paas, *Church Planting in the Secular West* (Grand Rapids, MI: Eerdmans, 2016), 219.

2. John Calvin, *Tracts and Treatises on the Reformation of the Church*, trans. Henry Beveridge, vol. 1 (Grand Rapids, MI: Eerdmans, 1958), 117.

3. R. M. Kingdon, T. A. Lambert, and I. M. Watt, eds., *The Registers of the Consistory of Geneva at the Time of Calvin*, vol. 1 (Grand Rapids, MI: Eerdmans, 2000), 45–46.

4. *French Confession of 1559*, trans. Ellen Babinski and Joseph Small (Louisville, KY: Presbyterian Church (U.S.A.), 1998), para. 22.

5. Service for the Lord's Day, *Book of Common Worship* (Louisville, KY: Westminster John Knox Press, 1993), 54.

6. French Confession of 1559, para. 29.

7. John Climacus, *The Ladder of Divine Ascent* (Mahwah, NJ: Paulist Press, 1982), 93.

8. See Thomas F. Torrance, *Conflict and Agreement in the Church*, vol. 1 (Eugene, OR: Wipf & Stock, 1996), 97.

9. St. Cyprian of Carthage, "The Unity of the Catholic Church," in *On the Church: Select Treatises*, trans. Allen Brent (Crestwood, NY: St. Vladimir's Seminary Press, 2006), 157.

10. The college of bishops to which Cyprian appeals forms the patristic foundation for Calvin's vision of the presbytery.

11. Christina Cleveland, *Disunity in Christ: Uncovering the Hidden Forces That Keep Us Apart* (Downers Grove, IL: InterVarsity Press 2013), 97.

12. Ibid.

13. John V. Taylor, *The Go-Between God* (St. Alban's Place, UK: SCM Press, 1972), 64.

14. Ibid., 107

15. Dietrich Bonhoeffer, *Life Together* (San Francisco: Harper, 1954), 26.

16. "Participants in 1001 Movement Are Young, Racially Diverse," April 27, 2015, http://www.pcusa.org/news/2015/4/27/participants-1001-movement-are-young-racially-dive.

17. See the observations regarding millennials and evangelism in Angie Andriot, Deb Coe, and Vera White, *Final Report: 1001 NWC Conference Interviews*, PC(USA) Research Services report, http://www.presbyterianmission.org/site_media/media/uploads/1001/pdfs/1001_nwc_conference_report.pdf.

9. Communities Sustainability

1. "Church Planters and the Cost of Starting a Church," April 26, 2016, https://www.barna.com/research/church-planters-and-the-cost-of-starting-a-church.

2. "Community Practices," The Open Door, http://pghopendoor.org/about-the-open-door/community-practices.

3. Angie Andriot, Deb Coe, and Vera White, *Final Report: Worshiping Community Leaders Survey*, April 2015, PC(USA) Research Services report, https://www.pcusa.org/site_media/media/uploads/1001/pdfs/worshiping-community-leaders-survey.pdf, 5.

4. *Church Growth Research Project, Report on Strand 3b: An Analysis of Fresh Expressions of Church and Church Plants Begun in the Period 1992–2012*, October 2013, Church Army's Research Unit report, http://www.churchgrowthresearch.org.uk/UserFiles/File/Reports/churchgrowthresearch_freshexpressions.pdf.

5. Kristine Miller and Scott McKenzie, *Bounty: Ten Ways to Increase Giving at Your Church* (Nashville: Abingdon Press, 2013), 17–19.

6. Scott Simmons, mission developer of LydiaPlace Collaborative Communities in St. Paul, Minnesota, outlines various mechanisms of funding upstart ministries at http://www.luthersem.edu/stewardship/default.aspx?m=6667&post=4497.

10. The Future of New Worshiping Communities

1. *Project Blueprint, 1001 New Worshiping Communities* (Louisville, KY: Research Services, Presbyterian Church (U.S.A.), 2014).

2. "Videos Stories," https://www.presbyterianmission.org/ministries/1001-2/about-1001/videos.

3. *1001 NWC Leaders Report*, February 2017, PC(USA) Research Services report, https://www.presbyterianmission.org/wp-content/uploads/1001-NWC-final-report-with-appendices.pdf, 20.

4. Ibid., 6.

5. Ibid., 7.

6. Ibid., 22.

7. Ibid., 4.

8. Ibid., 29.

9. Ibid., 19.

10. Ibid.

11. *Final Report: Worshiping Community Leaders Survey*, April 2015, PC(USA) Research Services report, https://www.pcusa.org/site_media/media /uploads/1001/pdfs/worshiping-community-leaders-survey.pdf, 15.

12. *1001 NWC Leaders Report*, 19.

13. Ibid., 11.

14. Ibid., 12.

15. Ibid., 15.

16. Ibid., 23.

17. Ibid., 29–30. The study used the following definitions for the forms of evangelism:

Intellectual: Communicating the gospel and engaging in theological discussions of truth and meaning; inviting questions of faith.

Invitational: Communicating a message of open doors by welcoming all regardless of background or lifestyle.

Testimonial: Sharing the Good News and telling your "God story."

Missional: Engaging in acts of mission as a way to demonstrate God's love.

Relational: Forming relationships with non-Christians as a way to share God's love.

18. *Starting New Worshiping Communities: A Process of Discernment*, February 2010, Presbyterian Mission resource, https://www.presbyterianmission.org /resource/starting-new-churches.

19. Michael Moynagh, *Church in Life: Innovation, Mission, and Ecclesiology* (London: SCM Press, 2017), 9.

20. Ibid.

CPSIA information can be obtained
at www.ICGtesting.com
Printed in the USA
FSOW02n0119080118
42896FS

9 780664 263096